CLASSIC SERMONS
ON
FAITH AND DOUBT

KREGEL CLASSIC SERMONS Series

Classic Sermons on Suffering
Classic Sermons on Faith and Doubt
Classic Sermons on Prayer

CLASSIC SERMONS ON FAITH AND DOUBT

Compiled by
Warren W. Wiersbe

KREGEL PUBLICATIONS
Grand Rapids, Michigan 49501

Library of Congress Cataloging in Publication Data

Warren W. Wiersbe (compiler)
Classic Sermons on Faith and Doubt

(Kregel Classic Sermons Series)
Bibliography: p.
Includes index.
1. Faith—Sermons. 2. Sermons, American.
3. Sermons, English. I. Wiersbe, Warren W. II. Title.
III. Series: Kregel Classic Sermons Series.
BT771.2.C57 1985 252 85-9767
ISBN 0-8254-4028-9

2 3 4 5 6 Printing/Year 91 90 89 88 87

Printed in the United States of America

Dedicated to the memory of

DR. D. MARTYN LLOYD-JONES
(1895-1981)

He was a peerless expositor of the Word who in his life and preaching was a model of the highest ideals in ministry.

He had time for young preachers, and we shall always be grateful for the instruction and encouragement that he shared.

"And when the chief Shepherd shall appear, ye shall receive a crown of glory that fadeth not away" (1 Peter 5:4).

Dedicated to the memory of

CONTENTS

PREFACE

THE *CLASSIC SERMONS SERIES* is an attempt to assemble and publish meaningful sermons from master preachers about significant themes.

These are *sermons,* not essays or chapters taken from books about themes. Not all of these sermons could be called "great," but all of them are *meaningful.* They apply the truths of the Bible to the needs of the human heart, which is something that all effective preaching must do.

While some are better known than others, all of the preachers, whose sermons I have selected, had important ministries and were highly respected in their day. The fact that a sermon is included in this volume does not mean that either the compiler or the publisher agrees with or endorses everything that the man did, preached, or wrote. The sermon is here, because it has a valued contribution to make.

These are sermons about *significant* themes. The pulpit is no place to play with trivia. The preacher has thirty minutes in which to help mend broken hearts, change defeated lives, and save lost souls; and he can never accomplish this demanding ministry by distributing homiletical tid-bits. In these difficult days, we do not need "clever" pulpiteers who discuss the times; we need dedicated ambassadors who will preach the eternities.

The reading of these sermons can enrich your own spiritual life. The studying of them can enrich your own skills as an interpreter and expounder of God's truth. However God uses these sermons in your own life and ministry, my prayer is that His Church around the world will be encouraged and strengthened.

Back to the Bible Broadcast
Lincoln, Nebraska

WARREN W. WIERSBE

Anxious Care

Alexander Maclaren (1826-1910) was one of Great Britain's most famous preachers. While pastoring the Union Chapel, Manchester (1858-1903), he became known as "the prince of expository preachers." Rarely active in denominational or civic affairs, Maclaren invested his time studying the Word in the original and sharing its truths with others in sermons that are still models of effective expository preaching. He published a number of books of sermons and climaxed his ministry by publishing his monumental *Expositions of Holy Scripture.* This message is taken from *Sermons Preached in Manchester,* published by Funk and Wagnalls Company (1902).

Alexander Maclaren

1

ANXIOUS CARE

Ye cannot serve God and Mammon. Therefore I say unto you, Take no thought for your life (Matthew 6:24-25).

FORESIGHT AND FOREBODING are two very different things. It is not that the one is the exaggeration of the other, but the one is opposed to the other. The more a man looks forward, in the exercise of foresight, the less he does so in the exercise of foreboding. And the more he is tortured by anxious thoughts about a *possible* future, the less clear vision has he of a *likely* future, and the less power to influence it. When Christ here, therefore, enjoins the abstinence from thought for our life and for the future, it is not for the sake of getting away from the pressure of a very unpleasant command that we say, He does not mean to prevent the exercise of wise and provident foresight and preparation for what is to come. When this English version of the Bible was made, the phrase "taking thought" meant solicitous anxiety, and that is the true rendering and proper meaning of the original. The idea is, therefore, that here there is forbidden for a Christian, not the careful preparation for what is likely to come, not the foresight of the storm, and taking in sail while yet there is time, but the constant occupation and distraction of the heart with gazing forward, and fearing, and being weakened thereby; or, to come back to words already used, foresight is commanded, and, *therefore,* foreboding is forbidden. My only object now, is to endeavor to gather together by their link of connection, the whole of those precepts which follow my text to the close of the chapter; and to try to set before you, in the order in which they stand, and in their organic connection with each other, the reasons which Christ gives for the absence of anxious care from our minds.

I mass them all into three. If you notice, the whole section, to the end of the chapter, is divided into three parts, by the threefold repetition of the injunction, "Take no thought." *"Take no thought for your life, what ye shall eat, or what ye shall drink; nor yet for your body, what ye shall put on."* The reason for the command as given in this first section follows: — *Is not the life more than meat, and the body than raiment?* The expansion of that runs on to the close of the thirtieth verse.

Then there follows another division or section of the whole, marked by the repetition of the command, *"Take no thought,"* saying, *"What shall we eat? or, What shall we drink: or, Wherewithal shall we be clothed?"* The reason given for the command in this second section is *"for after all these things do the Gentiles seek. For your heavenly Father knoweth that ye have need of all these things. But seek ye first the kingdom of God."* (vv. 31-33).

And then follows a third section marked by the third repetition of the command, *"Take no thought for the morrow."* The reason given for the command in this third section is *"for the morrow shall take thought for the things of itself."*

Now if we try to generalize the lessons that lie in these three great divisions of the Sermon on the Mount, we get these: anxious thought is contrary to all the lessons of nature, which show it to be unnecessary. That is the first, the longest section. Then, secondly, anxious thought is contrary to all the lessons of revelation or religion, which show it to be heathenish. And lastly, anxious thought is contrary to the whole scheme of Providence, which shows it to be futile. You do not *need* to be anxious. It is *wicked* to be anxious. It is *of no use* to be anxious. These are the three things, contrary to the lessons of Nature; contrary to the great principles of the Gospel; and contrary to the scheme of Providence. Let us try now simply to follow the course of thought in our Lord's illustration of these three principles.

Anxiety Is Contrary to Nature

The first is the consideration of the teaching of nature.

"Take no thought for your life, what ye shall eat, or what ye shall drink; nor yet for your body, what ye shall put on. Is not the life more than meat, and the body than raiment?" (Matthew 6:25). And then comes the illustration of the fowls of the air and the lilies of the field.

The whole of these four or five verses fall into these general thoughts: *You are obliged to trust God for your body, for its structure, for its form, for its habitudes, and for the length of your being;* you are obliged to trust Him for the foundation—trust Him for the superstructure. You are obliged to trust Him, whether you will or not, for the greater—trust Him gladly for the less. You cannot help being dependent. After all your anxiety, it is only directed to the providing of the things that are needful for life. Life itself, though it be a natural thing, comes direct from God's hand, and all that you can do, with all your carking cares, and laborious days, and sleepless nights, is but to adorn a little more beautifully or a little less beautifully, the allotted span, and to feed a little more delicately or a little less delicately, the body which God has given you! What is the use of being careful for food and raiment, when down below these necessities there lies the awful question—for the answer to which you have to hang helpless, in implicit, powerless dependence upon God—Shall I live, or shall I die? Shall I have a body instinct with vitality, or a body crumbling amidst the clods of the valley?

After all your work, your anxiety gets but such a little way down; like some passing shower of rain, that only softens the hard-baked surface of the soil, and has nothing to do with fructifying the seed that lies inches below the reach of its useless moisture. Anxious care is *foolish;* for far beyond the region within which your anxieties move, there is the greater region in which there must be entire dependence upon God. "Is not the life more than meat? Is not the body more than raiment?" You *must* trust Him for that; you may as well trust Him for all the rest.

Then, again, there comes up this other thought: Not only are you compelled to exercise un-anxious dependence in regard to a matter which you cannot influence—the life of the body—and that is the greater; but, still further, *God gives you that.* Very well, *God gives you the greater; and God's great gifts are always inclusive of God's little gifts.* When He bestows the thing, He bestows all the consequences of the thing as well. When He gives a life, He swears by the gift that He will give what is needful to sustain it. God does not stop halfway in any of His bestowments. He gives royally and liberally, honestly and sincerely, logically and completely. When He bestows a life, therefore, you may be quite sure that He is not going to stultify His own gift by retaining unbestowed anything that is wanted for its blessing and its power. You have had to trust Him for the greater; trust Him for the less. He has given you the greater; no doubt He will give you the less. "The life is more than meat, and the body than raiment." "Which of you by taking thought can add one cubit unto his stature? And why take ye thought for raiment?"

Then there is another thought. *Look at God's ways of doing with all His creatures.* The animate and the inanimate creation are appealed to, the fowls of the air and the lilies of the field, the one in reference to food and the other in reference to clothing, which are the two great wants already spoken of by Christ in the previous verses. I am not going to linger on the exquisite beauty of these illustrations. Every sensitive heart and pure eye dwells upon them with delight. The "fowls of the air," "the lilies of the field," "they toil not, neither do they spin;" and then, with what an eye for the beauty of God's universe—"Solomon, in all his glory, was not arrayed like one of these!" Now, what is the force of this consideration? It is this: There is a specimen, in an inferior creation, of the same principles which *you* can trust, you men who are "better than they." And not only that: There is an instance, not only of God's giving things that are necessary, but of God's giving more, lavishing *beauty* upon the flowers of the field. I do not think that we sufficiently dwell upon the moral and spiritual uses of beauty in God's universe. That everywhere His loving, wooing hand should touch the flower into grace, and deck all barren places with glory and with fairness—what does *that* reveal to us about Him? It says to us, He does not give scantily: it is not the mere measure of what is wanted, absolutely needed, to support a bare existence, that God bestows. He taketh pleasure in the prosperity of His servants.

Joy, love, and beauty belong to Him; and the smile upon His face that comes from the contemplation of His own fairness flung out into His glorious creation, is a prophecy of the gladness that comes into His heart from His own holiness and more ethereal beauty adorning the spiritual creatures whom He has made to flash back His likeness. The flowers of the field are so clothed that we may learn the lesson, that it is a fair Spirit, a loving Spirit, a bountiful Spirit, and a royal heart that presides over the bestowments of creation, and allots gifts to men.

But notice, further, how much of the force of what Christ says here, depends on the consideration of *the inferiority of these creatures who are thus blessed; and also notice what are the particulars of that inferiority.* We read that verse, "They sow not, neither do they reap, nor gather into barns," as if it marked out a particular in which their free and untoilsome lives were superior to ours. It is the very opposite. It is part of the thing that marks them as lower than we, that they have not to work for the future. They reap not, they sow not, they gather not; are ye not much better than they? Better in this, among other things, that God has given us the privilege of influencing the future by our faithful toil, by the sweat of our brow, and by the labor of our hands. These creatures labor not, and yet they are fed. The lesson for us is how much more may we, whom God has blessed with the power of work and gifted with force to mold the future, be sure that He will bless the exercise of the prerogative by which He exalts us above inferior creatures, and makes us capable of toil.

You can influence tomorrow. What you can influence by work, fret not about, for you *can* work. What you cannot influence by work, fret not about, for it is vain. "They toil not, neither do they spin." You are lifted above them because God has given you hands, that can grasp the tool or the pen. Man's crown of glory, as well as man's curse and punishment, is "in the sweat of thy brow shalt thou eat bread." So learn what you have to do with that great power of anticipation! It is meant to be the *guide of wise work.* It is meant to be the support for far-reaching, strenuous action. It is meant to elevate us above mere living from hand to mouth; to ennoble the whole being by leading to and directing toil that is blessed, because there is no anxiety in it, labor that will be successful, since it is according to the will of that God who has endowed us with the power of putting it forth.

Then there comes another inferiority. *"Your heavenly Father* feedeth them." They cannot say *"Father!"* and yet they are fed. You are above them by the prerogative of toil. You are above them by the nearer relation which you sustain to your Father in heaven. He is their Maker, and lavishes His goodness upon them, He is your Father, and He will not forget His child. *They* cannot trust, *you* can. *They* might be anxious, if they could look forward, for they know not the hand that feeds them; but *you* can turn around, and recognize the source of all blessings. So doubly ought you to be guarded from care by the lesson of that free joyful nature that lies around about you, and say, No fear of famine, nor of poverty, nor of want; for He feedeth the ravens when they cry. No reason for distrust! Shame on me if I am anxious! For every lily of the field blows its beauty, and every bird of the air carols its song without sorrowful foreboding, and yet there is no *Father* in the heaven to them!

And the last inferiority is this: *"Today it is, and tomorrow it is cast into the oven."* Their little life is thus blessed and brightened. Oh, how much greater will be the mercies that belong to them who have a longer life upon earth, and who never die! The lesson is not—these are the plebeians in God's universe, and you are the aristocracy, and you may trust Him; but it is—they, by their inferior place, have lesser and lower wants, wants but for a bounded being, wants that stretch not beyond earthly existence, and that for a brief span. They are blessed in the present, for the oven tomorrow saddens not the blossoming today. You have nobler necessities and higher longings, wants that belong to a soul that never dies, to a nature which may glow with the consciousness that God is your Father, wants which "look before and after," therefore, you are "better than they;" and "shall He not much more clothe you, O ye of little faith?"

Anxiety Is Contrary to Revelation

And now, in the second place, there is here another general line of considerations tending to dispel all anxious care—the thought that *it is contrary to all the lessons of Religion, or Revelation, which show it to be heathenish.* There are three clauses devoted to the illustration of this thought: "After all these things do the Gentiles seek. For your heavenly Father knoweth that ye have need of all these things. But seek ye first the kingdom of God, and His righteousness, and all these things shall be added unto you" (Matthew 6:32-33).

The first contains the principle, that *solicitude for the future is at heart heathen worldly-mindedness.* The heathen tendency in us all leads to an over-estimate of material good, and it is a question of circumstances whether that shall show itself in heaping up earthly treasures or in anxious care. They are the same plant, only the one is growing in the tropics of sunny prosperity, and the other in the arctic zone of chill penury. The one is the sin of the worldly-minded rich man, the other is the sin of the worldly-minded poor man. The character is the same turned inside out! And, therefore, the words "ye cannot serve God and mammon," stand in this chapter in the center between our Lord's warning against laying up treasures on earth, and His warnings against being full of cares for earth. He would show us thereby that these two apparently opposite states of mind in reality spring from that one root, and are equally, though differently, "serving mammon." We do not sufficiently reflect upon that. We say, perhaps, this intense solicitude of ours is a matter of temperament, or of circumstances. So it may be; but the Gospel was sent to help us to cure worldly temperaments, and to master circumstances. But *the* reason why we are troubled and careful about the things of this life, lies here, that our hearts have got an earthly direction, that we are at heart heathenish in our lives, and in our desires. It is the very characteristic of the Gentile (that is to say, of the heathen) that earth should bound his horizon. It is the very characteristic of the worldly man that all his anxieties on the one hand, and all his joys on the other, should be "cribbed, cabined, and confined" within the narrow sphere of the Visible. When a Christian is living in the foreboding of some earthly sorrow to come down upon him, and is feeling as if there would be nothing left if some earthly treasure were swept away, is it not, in the very root of it, idolatry, worldly-mindedness? Is it not clean contrary to all our profession that for us "there is none upon earth that we desire besides Thee"? Anxious care rests upon a basis of heathen worldly-mindedness.

Anxious care rests upon a basis, too, of heathen misunderstanding of the character of God. "Your heavenly Father knoweth that you have need of all these things." The heathen thought of God is that He is far removed from our perplexities, either ignorant of our struggles, or unsympathizing with them. The Christian has the double armor against anxiety: the name of the Father, and the conviction that the Father's knowledge is co-extensive with the Father's love. He who calls us His children thoroughly understands what His children want. And so, anxiety is contrary to the very name by which we have learned to call God, and to the pledge of pitying care and perfect knowledge of our frame which lies in the words "our Father." Our Father is the name of God, and our Father intensely cares for us, and lovingly does all things for us.

And then, still further, Christ points out here, not only what is the real root of this solicitous care—something very like worldly-mindedness—heathen worldly-mindedness; but He points out what is the one counterpoise of it—*seek first the kingdom of God.* It is of no use only to tell men that they *ought* to trust, that the birds of the air might teach them to trust, that the flowers of the field might preach resignation and confidence to them. It is of no use to attempt to scold them into trust, by telling them that distrust is heathenish! You must fill the heart with a supreme and transcendent desire after the one supreme object; and then there will be no room and leisure left for the anxious care after the lesser. Have inwrought into your being, Christian man, the opposite of that heathen overregard for earthly things. "Seek first the kingdom of God." Let all your spirit be stretching itself out towards that Divine and blessed reality, longing to be a subject of that kingdom, and a possessor of that righteousness; and "the cares that infest the day" shall steal away from out of the sacred pavilion of your believing spirit. Fill your heart with desires after what is worthy of desire; and the greater having entered in, all lesser objects will rank themselves in the right place, and the "glory that excelleth" will outshine the seducing brightness of the paltry present. Oh, it is want of love, it is want of earnest desire, it is want of firm conviction that God, God only, God by Himself, is enough for me, that make me careful and troubled. And, therefore, if I could only attain unto that sublime and calm height of perfect conviction, that He is sufficient for me, that He is with me forever—the satisfying object of my desires and the glorious reward of my searchings, let life and death come as they may; let riches, poverty, health, sickness, all the antitheses of human circumstances storm down upon me in quick alternation, yet in them all I shall be content and peaceful. God is beside me! And His presence brings in its train whatsoever things I need. You cannot cast out the sin of foreboding thoughts by any power short of the entrance of Christ and His love. The blessings of faith and felt communion leave no room nor leisure for anxiety.

Anxiety Is Contrary to Providence

Finally, Christ here tells us, that thought for the morrow is *contrary to all the scheme of Providence, which shows it to be vain.* "The morrow shall take thought for the things of itself. Sufficient unto the day is the evil thereof" (Matthew 6:34).

I interpret these two clauses as meaning this: Tomorrow has anxieties enough of its own, after and in spite of all the anxieties about it today by which you try to free it from care when it comes. *Every* day, every day will have its evil, have it to the end. And every day will have evil enough for all the strength that a man has to cope with it. Thus it just comes to this: Anxiety, it is all vain. After all your careful watching for the corner of the heaven where the cloud is to come from, there *will be* a cloud, and it will rise somewhere, but you never know in what quarter. The morrow shall have its own anxieties. After all your fortifying of the castle of your life, there will be some little postern left unguarded, some little weak place in the wall left uncommanded by a battery; and there, where you never looked for him, the inevitable invader will come in! After all the plunging of the hero in the fabled waters that made him invulnerable, there was the little spot on the heel, and the arrow found its way *there!* There is nothing certain to happen, says the proverb, but the unforeseen. Tomorrow *will have* its cares, spite of anything that anxiety and foreboding can do. It is God's law of Providence that a man shall be disciplined by sorrow; and to try to escape from that law by any forecasting prudence, is utterly hopeless, and madness.

And what does your anxiety do? It does not empty tomorrow of its sorrows; but, oh, it empties today of its strength. It does not make you escape the evil, it makes you unfit to cope with it when it comes. It does not bless tomorrow, and it robs today. For every day has its own burden. Sufficient for each day is the evil which properly belongs to it. Do not add tomorrow's to today's. Do not drag the future into the present. The present has enough to do with its own proper concerns. We have always strength to bear the evil when it comes. We have not strength to bear the foreboding of it. As thy day, so thy strength shall be. In strict proportion to the existing exigencies will be the God-given power; but if you cram and condense today's sorrows by experience, and tomorrow's sorrows by anticipation, into the narrow round of the one twenty-four hours, there is no promise that as *that* day thy strength shall be! God gives us power to bear all the sorrows of His making; but He does not give us power to bear the sorrows of our own making, which *the anticipation* of sorrow most assuredly is.

Then, contrary to the lessons of nature, contrary to the teachings of religion, contrary to the scheme of Providence—weakening your strength, distracting your mind, sucking the sunshine out of every landscape, and casting a shadow over all the beauty—the curse of our lives is that heathenish, blind, useless, faithless, needless anxiety in which we *do* indulge. Look forward, for God has given you that royal and wonderful gift of dwelling in the future, and bringing all its glories around your present. Look forward, not for life, but for heaven; not for food and raiment, but for the righteousness after which it is blessed to hunger and thirst, and wherewith it is blessed to be clothed. Not for earth, but for heaven, let your forecasting gift of prophecy come into play. Fill the present with quiet faith, with patient waiting, with honest work, with wise reading of God's lessons of nature, of providence, and of grace, all of which say to us, Live in God's future, that the present may be bright; and work in the present, that the future may be certain! *They* may well look around in expectation, sunny and unclouded, of a blessed time to come, whose hearts are already "fixed, trusting in the Lord." He to whom there is a present Christ, and a present Spirit, and a present Father, and a present forgiveness, and a present redemption, may well live expiating in all the glorious distance of the unknown to come, sending out from his placid heart over all the weltering waters of this lower world, the peaceful seeking dove, his meek Hope, that shall come back again from its flight with some palm-branch broken from the trees of Paradise between its bill. And he that has *no* such present, *has* a future, dark, chaotic, heaving with its destructive ocean; and over it there goes forever—black-pinioned, winging its solitary and hopeless flight, the raven of his anxious thoughts, and finds no place to rest, and comes back again to the desolate ark with its foreboding croak of evil in the present and evil in the future. Live in Christ, "the same yesterday, and today, and forever," and *His* presence shall make all *your* past, present, and future—memory, enjoyment, and hope—to be bright and beautiful, because all are centered in Him!

NOTES

Dealing With Doubt

Henry Drummond (1851-1897) was trained as an instructor in natural science and taught in his native Scotland, eventually becoming professor at the Free Church College, Glasgow. Influenced by Dwight L. Moody, Drummond developed into an effective personal worker and evangelist to the students, and was greatly used to win many to Christ. He is best known for his address on 1 Corinthians 13, "The Greatest Thing in the World." This message is taken from *The Greatest Thing in the World and Other Addresses,* published in 1898 by Fleming H. Revell Company.

Henry Drummond

2

DEALING WITH DOUBT

THERE IS A subject which I think workers among young men cannot afford to keep out of sight. I mean the subject of "Doubt." We are forced to face that subject. We have no choice. I would rather let it alone; but every day of my life I meet men who doubt, and I am quite sure that most Christian workers among men have innumerable interviews every year with men who raise skeptical difficulties about religion.

Now it becomes a matter of great practical importance that we should know how to deal wisely with these. Upon the whole, I think these are the best men in the country. I speak of the universities with which I am familiar, and I say that the men who are perplexed—the men who come to you with serious and honest difficulties—are the best men. They are men of intellectual honesty, and cannot allow themselves to be put to rest by words, or phrases, or traditions, or theologies, but who must get to the bottom of things for themselves. And if I am not mistaken, Christ was very fond of these men. The outsiders always interested Him, and touched Him. The orthodox people—the Pharisees—He was much less interested in. He went with publicans and sinners, with people who were in revolt against the respectability, intellectual and religious, of the day. And following Him, we are entitled to give sympathetic consideration to those whom He loved and took trouble with.

First, let me mention something about

The Origin of Doubt

In the first place, *we are born questioners.* Look at the wonderment of a little child in its eyes before it can speak. The child's great word when it begins to speak is, "Why?" Every child is full of every kind of question, about every kind of thing, that moves, and shines, and changes, in the little world in which it lives.

That is the incipient doubt in the nature of man. Respect doubt for its origin. It is an inevitable thing. It is not a thing to be crushed. It is a part of man as God made him. Heresy is truth in the making, and doubt is the prelude of knowledge.

Secondly, *the world is a Sphinx.* It is a vast riddle—an unfathomable mystery—and on every side there is temptation to questioning. In every leaf, in every cell of every leaf, there are a hundred problems. There are ten good years of a man's life in investigating what is in a leaf, and there are five good years more in investigating the things that are in the things that are in the leaf. God has planned the world to incite men to intellectual activity.

Thirdly, *the instrument with which we attempt to investigate truth is impaired.* Some say it fell, and the glass is broken. Some say prejudice, heredity, or sin, have spoiled its sight, and have blinded our eyes and deadened our ears. In any case the instruments with which we work upon truth, even in the strongest men, are feeble and inadequate to their tremendous task.

And in the fourth place, *all religious truths are doubtable.* There is no absolute truth for any one of them. Even that fundamental truth—the existence of a God—no man can prove by reason. The ordinary proof for the existence of God involves either an assumption, argument in a circle, or a contradiction. The impression of God is kept up by experience, not by logic. And hence, when the experimental religion of a man, of a community, or of a nation wanes, religion wanes—their idea of God grows indistinct, and that man, community or nation becomes infidel.

Bear in mind, then, that all religious truths are doubtable, even those which we hold most strongly.

What does this brief account of the origin of doubt teach us? It teaches us great intellectual humility. It teaches us sympathy and toleration with all men who venture upon the ocean of truth to find out a path through it for themselves. Do you sometimes feel yourself thinking unkind things about your fellow students who have intellectual difficulty? I know how hard it is always to feel sympathy and toleration for them; but we must address ourselves to that most carefully and most religiously. If my brother is short-sighted I must not abuse him or speak against him; I must pity him, and if possible try to improve his sight, or to make things that he is to look at so bright that he cannot help seeing. But never let us think evil of men who do not see as we do. From the bottom of our hearts let us pity them, and let us take them by the hand and spend time and thought over them, and try to lead them to the true light.

What has been

The Church's Treatment of Doubt

in the past? It has been very simple. "There is a heretic. Burn him!" That is all. "There is a man who has gone off the road. Bring him back and torture him!"

We have got past that physically; have we got past it morally? What does the modern church say to a man who is skeptical? Not "Burn him!" but "Brand him!" "Brand him!"—call him a bad name. And in many countries at the present time, a man who is branded as a heretic is despised, tabooed and put out of religious society, much more than if he had gone wrong in morals. I think I am speaking within the facts when I say that a man who is unsound is looked upon in many communities with more suspicion and with more pious horror than a man who now and then gets drunk. "Burn him!" "Brand him!" "Excommunicate him!" That has been the church's treatment of doubt, and that is perhaps to some extent the treatment which we ourselves are inclined to give to the men who cannot see the truths of Christianity as we see them.

Contrast

Christ's Treatment of Doubt

I have spoken already of His strange partiality for the outsiders—for the scattered heretics up and down the country; of the care with which He loved to deal with them, and of the respect in which He held their intellectual difficulties. Christ never failed to distinguish between doubt and unbelief. Doubt is *"can't believe";* unbelief is *"won't believe."* Doubt is honesty: unbelief is obstinacy. Doubt is looking for light; unbelief is content with darkness. Loving darkness rather than light—that is what Christ attacked, and attacked unsparingly. But for the intellectual questioning of Thomas, and Philip, and Nicodemus, and the many others who came to Him to have their great problems solved, He was respectful and generous and tolerant.

And how did He meet their doubts? The church, as I have said, says, "Brand him!" Christ said, "Teach him." He destroyed by fulfilling. When Thomas came to Him and denied His very resurrection, and stood before Him waiting for the scathing words and lashing for his unbelief, they never came. They never came! Christ gave him facts—facts! No man can go around facts. Christ said, "Behold My hands and My feet." The great god of science at the present time is a fact. It works with facts. Its cry is, "Give me facts. Found anything you like upon facts and we will believe it." The spirit of Christ was the scientific spirit. He founded His religion upon facts; and He asked all men to found their religion upon facts.

Now, get up the facts of Christianity, and take men to the facts. Theologies—and I am not speaking disrespectfully of theology; theology is as scientific a thing as any other science of facts—but theologies are human versions of Divine truths, and hence the varieties of the versions and the inconsistencies of them. I would allow a man to select whichever version of this truth he liked *afterwards;* but I would ask him to begin with no version, but go back to the facts and base his Christian life upon these.

That is the great lesson of the New Testament way of looking at doubt, of Christ's treatment of doubt. It is not "Brand him!", but lovingly, wisely and tenderly to teach him. Faith is never opposed to reason in the New Testament; it is opposed to sight. You will find that a principle worth thinking over. *Faith is never opposed to reason in the New Testament, but to sight.*

With these principles in mind as to the origin of

doubt, and as to Christ's treatment of it, how are we ourselves to deal with those who are in intellectual difficulty?

How to Deal With Doubters

In the first place, I think *we must make all the concessions to them that we conscientiously can.*

When a doubter first encounters you, he pours out a deluge of abuse of churches, and ministers, and creeds, and Christians. Nine-tenths of what he says is probably true. Make concessions. Agree with him. It does him good to unburden himself of these things. He has been cherishing them for years—laying them up against Christians, against the Church, and against Christianity; and now he is startled to find the first Christian with whom he has talked over the thing almost entirely agrees with him. We are, of course, not responsible for everything that is said in the name of Christianity; but a man does not give up medicine because there are quack doctors, and no man has a right to give up his Christianity because there are spurious or inconsistent Christians. Then, as I already said, creeds are human versions of Divine truths; and we do not ask a man to accept all the creeds, any more than we ask him to accept all the Christians. We ask him to accept Christ, and the facts about Christ and the words of Christ. You will find the battle is half won when you have endorsed the man's objections, and possibly added a great many more to the charges which he has against ourselves. These men are in revolt against the kind of religion which we exhibit to the world—against the cant that is taught in the name of Christianity. And if the men that have never seen the real thing—if you could show them that, they would receive it as eagerly as you do. They are merely in revolt against the imperfections and inconsistencies of those who represent Christ to the world.

Second, *beg them to set aside, by an act of will, all unsolved problems:* such as the problem of the origin of evil, the problem of the Trinity, the problem of the relation of human will and predestination, and so on—problems which have been investigated for thousands of years without result—ask them to set those problems aside as insoluble. In the meantime, just as a man who is studying mathematics may be asked to set aside the problem of squaring the circle, let him go on with what can be done, and what has been done, and leave out of sight the impossible.

You will find that will relieve the skeptic's mind of a great deal of unnecessary cargo that has been in his way.

Thirdly, *talking about difficulties, as a rule, only aggravates them.*

Entire satisfaction to the intellect is unattainable about any of the greater problems, and if you try to get to the bottom of them by argument, there is no bottom there; and therefore you make the matter worse. But I would say what is known, and what can be honestly, philosophically, and scientifically said about one or two of the difficulties that the doubter raises, just to show him that you can do it—to show him that you are not a fool—that you are not merely groping in the dark yourself, but you have found whatever basis is possible. But I would not go around all the doctrines. I would simply do that with one or two; because the moment you cut off one, a hundred other heads will grow in its place. It would be a pity if all these problems could be solved. The joy of the intellectual life would be largely gone. I would not rob a man of his problems, nor would I have another man rob me of my problems. They are the delight of life, and the whole intellectual world would be stale and unprofitable if we knew everything.

Fourthly, and this is the great point, *turn away from the reason and go into the man's moral life.*

I don't mean, go into his moral life and see if the man is living in conscious sin, which is the great blinder of the eyes—I am speaking now of honest doubt; but open a new door into the practical side of man's nature. Entreat him not to postpone life and his life's usefulness until he has settled the problems of the universe. Tell him those problems will never all be settled; that his life will be done before he has begun to settle them; and ask him what he is doing with his life meantime. Charge him with wasting his life and his usefulness; and invite him to deal with the moral and practical difficulties of the world, and leave the intellectual difficulties as he goes along. To spend time upon these is proving the less important before the more important; and, as the French say, "The good is the enemy of the best." It is a good thing to think; it is a better thing to work—it is a better thing to do good. And you have him there, you see. He can't get beyond that. You have to tell him, in fact, that there are two organs of knowledge: the one reason, the other obedience. And now tell him, as he has tried the first and found the little in it, just for a moment or two to join you in trying the second. And when he asks whom he is to obey, you tell him there is but One, and lead him to the great historical figure who calls all men to Him: the one perfect life—the one Savior of mankind—the one Light of the world. Ask him to begin to obey Christ; and, doing His will, he shall know of the doctrine whether it be of God.

That, I think, is about the only thing you can do with a man: to get him into practical contact with the needs of the world, and to let him lose his intellectual difficulties meantime. Don't ask him to give them up altogether. Tell him to solve them afterward one by one if he can, but meantime to give his life to Christ and his time to the kingdom of God. You fetch him completely around when you do that. You have taken him away from the false side of his nature, and to the practical and moral side of his nature; and for the first time in his life, perhaps, he puts things in their true place. He puts his nature in the relations in which it ought to be, and he then only begins to live. By obedience he will soon become a learner and pupil for himself, and Christ will teach him things, and he will find whatever problems are solvable gradually solved as he goes along the path of practical duty.

Now, let me, in closing, give an instance of how to deal with specific points.

The question of miracles is thrown at my head every second day:

"What do you say to a man when he says to you, 'Why do you believe in miracles?' "

I say, "Because I have seen them."

He asks, "When?"

I say, "Yesterday."

"Where?"

"Down such-and-such a street I saw a man who was a drunkard redeemed by the power of an unseen Christ and saved from sin. That is a miracle."

The best apologetic for Christianity is a Christian. That is a fact which the man cannot get over. There are fifty other arguments for miracles, but none so good as that you have seen them. Perhaps you are one yourself. But take a man and show him a miracle with his own eyes. Then he will believe.

NOTES

The Tragedy of Life Without Faith

George Campbell Morgan (1863-1945) was the son of a British Baptist preacher and preached his first sermon when he was thirteen years old. He had no formal training for the ministry, but his tireless devotion to the study of the Bible helped him to become one of the leading Bible teachers of his day. Rejected by the Methodists, he was ordained into the Congregational ministry. He was associated with Dwight L. Moody in the Northfield Bible conferences and as an itinerant Bible teacher. He is best known as the pastor of Westminster Chapel, London (1904-17 and 1933-35). During his second term there, he had Dr. D. Martyn Lloyd-Jones as his associate. He published more than 60 books and booklets, and his sermons are found in *The Westminster Pulpit* (London, Pickering and Inglis). This sermon is from Volume 9.

G. Campbell Morgan

3

THE TRAGEDY OF LIFE WITHOUT FAITH

> I had fainted, unless I had believed to see the goodness of the Lord in the Land of the living (Psalm 27:13).

THE PSALM FROM which our text is taken is a song of conflicting emotions, in which victory is on the side of the nobler. As we listen to the singer we discover the opposing forces at war within the soul. Faith opposes fear, joy strenuously contends with sorrow, songs resolutely lift themselves for the silencing of sighing.

The fear, the sorrow, the sighing are patent. Note the questions at the commencement of the Psalm which even though they be prefaced by affirmations of faith, reveal the assault of fear, ". . . Whom shall I fear? . . . of whom shall I be afraid?" (Psalm 27:1). Observe the tumult of circumstances as revealed in the phrases that run like a dirge through the Psalm. Evil doers came to seek and to eat up my flesh; mine adversaries and my foes. An host against me; war against me! The day of trouble! Mine enemies round about me! My father and my mother have forsaken me. Mine enemies, mine adversaries, false witnesses, such as breathe out cruelty! There can be no escape from the sense of the tumult and trouble in the midst of which the singer lived.

Nevertheless, the Psalm in its entirety has not made this impression upon the heart of man. It is preeminently a Psalm of faith, of joy, of song. Note the affirmations with which it opens. "The Lord is my light and my salvation . . . the Lord is the strength of my life")—or even better, more accurately—"the Lord is the [stronghold] of my life." Observe the affirmations answering the questions. My heart will not be afraid! I will be confident! Mine head shall be lifted up! I will sing, yea, I will sing!

Then observe, after the opening stanzas of praise, the prayer that breaks from the heart of the singer, and notice how, through the brief prayer, there throbs the note of perfect confidence mastering that of overwhelming pain!

> Hear, O Lord, when I cry with my voice; have mercy also upon me, and answer me. When Thou saidst, Seek ye My face, my heart said unto Thee; Thy face, Lord, will I seek. Hide not Thy face far from me; put not Thy servant away in anger. Thou hast been my help; leave me not, neither forsake me, O God of my salvation, When my father and my mother forsake me, then the Lord will take me up. Teach me Thy way, O Lord, and lead me in a plain path, because of mine enemies. Deliver me not over unto the will of mine enemies . . . For false witnesses are risen up against me, and such as breathe out cruelty (Psalm 27:7-12).

Finally consider the last stanza of the Psalm, marking well its appeal:

> Wait on the Lord; be of good courage, and He shall strengthen thine heart. Wait, I say, on the Lord (Psalm 27:14).

The spiritual experience revealed in this song is one which, I venture to affirm, we all most earnestly desire. The tumult of sorrow we know. Is the triumph possible? Is it possible to know triumph in the midst of such tumultuous circumstances of grief? We wonder, we question, we doubt. Our sorrows are so subtle, our pain is so poignant, our difficulties are so complex, our circumstances are so peculiar.

Well, let us consider the reason for this singer's triumph. It is, of course, declared in the opening affirmations:

> The Lord is my light and my salvation; . . .
> The Lord is the strength [stronghold] of my life. . . .

It is illustrated in many subsequent statements which I have already quoted. From the standpoint of the soul's experience, the secret is most forcefully revealed in the words of my text. "*I had fainted,* unless I had believed to see the goodness of the Lord in the land of the living" (v. 13).

A critical examination of the text seems at first destructive of its simplest meaning. You will observe that in the Revised Version and the Authorized, the first three words of verse 13 are italicized; "*I had fainted*. . ." In Miles Coverdale's translation, the phrase has yet more emphasis, "I should utterly have fainted, unless I had believed to see the goodness of the Lord in the land of the living." There also all of the words are italicized. These words constitute an exegetical gloss, introduced by the translators to fill up some gap, some hiatus, to complete the sense of the text. As a matter of fact we must omit them, if we are to be careful in our consideration of the text.

What have we left? "... Unless I had believed to see the goodness of the Lord in the land of the living." When we further examine the text, we find that the word "unless" is not found in some manuscripts; neither is it found in the Septuagint, in the Syriac, or in the Vulgate. In the manuscripts in which the word is found, in the Massoretic Text, it is dotted over and beneath, which suggests that it is a spurious word.

As to the first words, "*I had fainted,*" we certainly must omit them. The word "unless," I am not prepared to omit. The absence of it from some manuscripts is not conclusive evidence. As old E. W. Hengstenberg suggests with quaint humor, the Massorites evidently lost their feet at this point. The sense of the passage demands the word. The statement without it is incongruous, following as it does immediately after the words, "... false witnesses are risen up against me, and such as breathe out cruelty." When the word is retained the whole text becomes a gasp, an exclamation! It is an imperfect sentence, indeed, no sentence at all, but a cry which is almost a groan. It is completed by a revealing hiatus, an eloquent silence. "... Unless I had believed to see the goodness of the Lord in the land of the living!" Then the translators attempted to fill this gap, and inserted the words, "I had fainted," or "I had utterly fainted." I can understand why they put them in. They were trying to write what the man was thinking. He did not do so. He left the blank, suggesting a something that could not be expressed. "I had fainted!" Nay, verily, that is altogether too weak. The horror was greater than that. There are moments in which the soul cannot faint. That is the sense of my text. This man who sings so finely, whose music marches to major strains, all the while mastering the minor, pauses and reveals the deep secret of that major music in this half-finished exclamation: "... Unless I had believed to see the goodness of the Lord in the land of the living." The horror is too profound for words; the terror is too terrible for utterance. It is nameless.

This, then, is a brief word of wonderful unveiling of the soul's consciousness of some lonely singer in the long ago, perchance David, more probably Hezekiah, I know not—but of some soul who had been looking out upon life. Poetically referring to the thing upon which he looked by the phrase, "the land of the living," a phrase describing the earth as he saw it, the dwelling place of men; he said: "Unless I had seen more than the land of the living, unless I had believed to see the goodness of the Lord there—!"

Leaving from this moment the peculiarly personal notes of the Psalm, let us consider the essential thoughts of the text along two lines. First, the land of the living as it appears in itself; second, the land of the living as it appears in the light which is here described as the goodness of the Lord.

Tragedy of Life in the Land of the Living

First then, the land of the living as it appears in itself. We must introduce this line of meditation by reminding ourselves of the viewpoint. It is not that of childhood. Childhood never sees the land of the living as this man saw it. Childhood, thank God, is beneficently sheltered and cannot see the things that some of us see so clearly and so tragically today. No child looks tragically upon life. Oh God, must I not amend that to say no child ought to do so! I fear there are some children who do, but it is not the natural viewpoint of the child.

Once again, it is not the natural viewpoint of youth. As Browning sang, "Youth sees but half." Youth is only intended to see half. It has not yet seen life in its entirety.

This is the viewpoint of that which, for lack of a better term, I may describe as maturity, the viewpoint of the man or the woman who has been compelled to face all the facts of life, who has passed through childhood's years with their sweetness and their softness, their laughter and their fun, who has gone beyond the golden age of youth, who has seen the colors fade upon the eastern sky and has tramped under the grey or under the blazing heat.

What, then, are the experiences of such? *The land of the living is to them the place of weakness.* There comes to us inevitably sooner or later this overwhelming sense of inability. We look back over the pathway we have traveled. We look at the things we have done, and looking back, we note how imperfect they all have been. We look carefully at the things we are doing today, and the sense of imperfection is even more appalling in the presence of immediate service than when we look at that which has been rendered. Then, ah, then, we look on, and there are so many things to be done which we shall never do, intentions that will never be fulfilled, work that has to be dropped and left and cannot be carried out. Not that the work does not need doing, not that the intention was not glorious, not that the vision was untrue, but that we are unable to do it. The appalling sense of inability, incompetence, weakness!

The land of the living is the place of disappointment. The sense of disillusionment comes inevitably to the human soul. We become disappointed with ourselves; we become disappointed in others. We become disappointed in the matter of our hopes and our aspirations. Many of them are not realized; and those we do realize, are they ever what we thought they would be? Are we ever satisfied? Is it not so, that when we have climbed the mountain height upon which we set our eyes and towards which we have striven strenuously, we are disappointed because there stretches away beyond us other mountain heights shutting us in, and we have not reached the level we thought we should have reached when that mountain height was climbed.

The land of the living is the place of mystery. Oh, this tangle of human life, the injustice of things, the perplexing problems that fret the soul, the thousand questions that perpetually force themselves out of the agony of life and find no answer. By mystery are we hemmed in; we do not know; we cannot explain; and the sense grows upon us with the passing of the years.

The land of the living is the place of sin. I use the word resolutely. Employ any other term that may better help you. However much we may argue concerning it, and whatever philosophy we may employ to attempt to explain it, there is this appalling consciousness of that which is wrong, out of joint, and not out of joint merely, but diseased withal. The terrific sense of the presence of the poison, of its power, and its pollution.

Again, and let this be the last word in the dark and dreary outlook, *the land of the living is the place of death.* Death, indiscriminating, ruthless, ghastly! Do you tell me that you have lost your hatred of death? Then you are abnormal, and your abnormality is not the abnormality of health but of disease! Death is ghastly, death is hateful! Death, that touches the little child in its sweetness, and the child is gone! Death, that strikes down the standard-bearer at the head of the army and leaves a gap that cannot be filled! Death, that by some accident or catastrophe sweeps upon the soldiers of the Cross and the servants of sin alike and engulfs them together so that the place that knew them knows them no more.

Unless there is something more to say than all that, what a tragedy life is, what a horror! The land of the living, this life in the midst of which we find ourselves, without God, what does it mean? No final wisdom or knowledge; no adequate strength to deal with things; no authority that moves right onward toward a goal; no possibility of restoration. I do not wonder that this singer gasped out, "... Unless I had believed! ..."

The Goodness of God in the Land of the Living

But the gasp was but an interlude in a song. Let us then look again at the land of the living as it appears in the light of the goodness of the Lord. Immediately we are halted by a phrase that suggests a truth, "... the goodness of the Lord!" The truth suggested by the phrase is that of the Lord of goodness, the biblical conception of God, the conception of God which inspired this song, the conception which inspired all the songs of this great Psalter. Shining through the whole of them in their unveiling of the human soul is the light of the God of revelation, the God of the Bible.

Goodness is one of the richest words in our vocabulary if we will but interpret it by the teaching of the biblical revelation. A greater word than holiness is this, a finer word than righteousness, including both, but having other qualities, which suffuse them with light and tenderness and mercy. The Hebrew word here so translated means radical and fundamental rightness, but it was a word that was used and translated by other words, beauty, gladness, prosperity. The Lord of goodness is the Lord of all that is right, all that is beautiful, all that is glad, and all that makes for the true prosperity of human life. He is the Lord of goodness, for He is the fountain head from which all these things proceed and the means by which these things become real in the experience of the race.

What light does this fact of God fling upon this strange, weird, life of ours? How does it help us? In what sense does belief in this God turn the sighing into the song, the fear into faith, the sorrow into joy? What are the things that make the triumph note of a song like this that thrills with pain?

I affirm in the first place that in the light of this revelation we come to understand that *life is related to God, and therefore, it is greater than all its experiences;* creating their possibilities, but refusing to be exhausted in them. There is a saying of Jesus which we quote perpetually, and never perhaps without seeing some new light in it. "And this is age-abiding life"—that is, life which is the life of the age, which cannot be destroyed in an age, or exhausted in an age, which runs through the whole of them, and touches them, and changes them, but is not changed by them—"to know Thee, the only true God. . . ." Now mark what this means in the case of human life. In the light of this revelation I come to the profound consciousness that my life is greater than all its experiences.

Life itself, whatever mystery it may have to face, whatever pain it may have to endure, whatever darkness it may have to go through, whatever agony it may have to bear, whatever sins it may have to mourn, life is vast. It is a Divine creation, and it is thus to this very God of goodness. Therefore, all these experiences of life, being related to Him, take on a new meaning, have a new value and have a new suggestiveness.

I have said that the land of the living is the place of weakness, that we become conscious of inability. In the light of this revelation of man's relationship to God, we discover that *the sense of inability is a suggestion of possibility*. I cannot do these things, and yet they are things that are to be done and can be done. The fact that I have seen the vision of them is in itself worthwhile. Human life will be measured presently and ultimately not by what it has achieved, but by what it set itself out to achieve, which, if it but be related to God, it will achieve in spite of all the darkness and the apparent disappointment of the present hour. That I know my own weakness is a sign of my own power. That I know there are things I do not know is a sign of my capacity to know the things I do not know. When a man says, "I cannot know the Infinite," in that acknowledgment he confesses that he knows it. He cannot include all the facts that are within it within his present consciousness. But to recognize the Infinite is in some sense to know it. That is at once a demonstration of relationship to God and a result of relationship to God. It would be a dark day indeed for the race if men became satisfied with the things that they have done and the things they are doing and imagined that when they had done their piece of work, all work had forever been completed. It is this very sense of inability which becomes the inspiration of endeavor for it rises out of a sense of possibility.

Again, the experience of the land of the living as a place of disappointment is after all but *a demonstration of high possibilities to the man who has seen the face of God and rejoiced in the light*. Noble disappointment is a demonstration of the splendor of things seen although never realized. Are you disappointed with yourself tonight? Then know this, that if you have seen a vision of yourself which is finer and higher, in the seeing there was value. The goodness of the Lord in the land of the living is that which makes a man, broken and disappointed with himself, look up into the Face of Deity and resolutely and daringly say, "Thou wilt perfect that which concerneth me. If you take that away from me, then I despair in the midst of life. But leave me that, and,

> With spirit elate,
> The mire and the fog I press through,
> For heaven shines under the cloud
> Of the day that is after tomorrow."

If the land of the living be the place of mystery, to the man who has seen the goodness of the Lord in the land of the living or who believes to see the goodness of the Lord in the land of the living, *the very fact of mystery is but the expression of profounder things, greater and more glorious.* In the twilight of the Jewish dispensation, the great founder, the lawgiver, uttered words that are to us today fresh and wonderful because of their immediate value. "The secret things" are the things that fill the soul with fear, the things of that realm of mystery which lies about us in life; the problems that confront us; the questions we ask and no answer comes; the secret things! Well, what of them? "They belong to the Lord, and the revealed things are for us and for our children." When we believe to see the goodness of the Lord in the land of the living, we know that there are no secret things from Him, that what we know not, He knows, that what amazes us never amazes Him, that the things for which we find no solution lie naked and open to His vision. Then if there are things which assault us and we cannot understand why they are permitted, the fact that they are permitted no longer troubles us, for He has permitted them, and He can make no mistake. The whole problem of evil lies there illuminated, and there and there alone the heart can find its rest.

The land of the living is the land of sin. *The consciousness of sin is born of the conviction of holiness.* Apart from the conviction of holiness there is no consciousness of sin. Then let us remember that in the full biblical revelation of God, at the very heart and center of the awful holiness that appals us, there burns and flames the infinite compassion which becomes passion and acts there-through for the saving of sinning souls. Woe is me, I am a sinner! Unless I believe to see the goodness of the Lord in the land of the living! But believing that and seeing that and knowing God, then even my sin shall not make me afraid!

And what of death? Our protest against death is the protest of life, and our horror of death is the horror of health. But once we see the goodness of the Lord in the land of the living, we discover that *death is not in God's original intention for humanity.* The scientists may tell us it is but the fulfilment of the natural order. We affirm that it is the carrying out of an unnatural condition resulting from human sin, that there should not have been any place for death had there been no failure and no sin. The goodness of the Lord in the land of the living transfigures the sackcloth and declares that through death there is the life, and beyond death there is a resurrection. If you take these things away from me, then death is still a horror so terrible that the only relief from it is in itself. I am not surprised that men who lose the Face of God end their lives, ". . . unless I had believed to see the goodness of the Lord in the land of the living!" Without that light, life is not worthwhile; life is a tragedy. Blot out this God from the heavens, deny me the Deity of the Face that shines in human tenderness for the unveiling of the Divine, take this God of the Bible away from me, then life is some hideous mockery and sport of demons. Unless! Oh, the horror of it, the nameless horror of it! Fainted? Nay, the soul becomes too quick and alive, with very agony and despair, challenge and revolt, hot anger and rebellion, ever to faint. Rebellion against what? Against the tragedy, the weakness, the disappointment, the mystery, the sin, and the death, the whole dark outlook!

Ah, but we have believed to see the goodness of the Lord in the land of the living; we have believed because we have seen the goodness of the Lord in the land of the living, and we believe still to see the goodness of the Lord in the land of the living. We believe that all the things which in themselves fill the soul with fear are held in the grip and grasp of the Great Father of an infinite grace.

At last there will be some explanation of all the pain and the mystery and the disappointment.

The Attitude of the Soul

What then is to be the true attitude of the soul? Let the psalmist tell us as he ends his song.

"... Wait on the Lord." Or as the New American Standard Version has it, "... Wait for the Lord. Be strong, and let your heart take courage; yes, wait for the Lord" (Psalm 27:14).

Those who have seen the Face of God are those who have seen it in the Face of Jesus. This is the ultimate in the biblical revelation. Through all the Old Testament we have prophecies, hopes, gleams of light, rosy flecks of a dawn yet to be. If we are to view God's brightest glory, we must look in Jesus' Face! To the soul who has seen the Face of God in the Face of Jesus, faith is forever against fear, joy lays hold upon sorrow, and songs rise up against sighing.

What then is the condition? Wait! There is nothing more difficult to do. *It is much easier to work for God than to wait for God.* To dare in active service is a far less wearisome thing than to wait, and yet by waiting the victory comes as well as the vision.

Moses, nurtured in the Court of Pharaoh, came to an hour when there was born within him a passion to deliver. What was his mistake? The mistake of imagining that in the hour when that passion was born, he was able to do the thing he desired to do. He had to wait for forty years. He always had to wait. In the hour of the wondrous deliverance, when by plague and judgment God set His people free, Moses did no other than wait. It is by waiting upon the Lord that the victory will be won. His goodness will be seen in the land of the living in proportion as His people wait upon Him.

I repeat as I finish, that this outlook is not that of childhood, and the final message is not for the child; the outlook is not that of youth, and the final message is not for youth.

The outlook is that of the men and women who have looked at life, looked at it all, and who if they have had nothing other to look at than life, have gasped with horror and been faint with fear! If such have believed to see the goodness of the Lord, then He teaches them this lesson, that in their waiting, they give Him His opportunity to work. He worketh for him that waiteth for Him.

NOTES

Faith on Trial: The Problem Stated

David Martyn Lloyd-Jones (1895-1981) was trained to be a doctor, but he felt a call to ministry in 1927 and accepted a Presbyterian church in his native Wales. G. Campbell Morgan hand-picked Lloyd-Jones to succeed him at Westminster Chapel, London; and "the Doctor's" strong expository ministry drew large congregations, particularly to the Friday Night Bible Class. Calvinistic in doctrine and classically Puritan in his homiletical style, Lloyd-Jones has left an indelible mark on preachers and preaching in the twentieth century. This message is chapter 1 of *Faith on Trial,* an exposition of Psalm 73, published by Baker Book House.

David Martyn Lloyd-Jones

4

FAITH ON TRIAL: THE PROBLEM STATED

> Truly God is good to Israel, even to such as are of a clean heart. But as for me, my feet were almost gone; my steps had well nigh slipped (Psalm 73:1-2).

THE GREAT VALUE of the Book of Psalms is that in it we have godly men stating their experience, and giving us an account of things that have happened to them in their spiritual life and warfare. Throughout history the Book of Psalms has, therefore, been a book of great value for God's people. Again and again it provides them with the kind of comfort and teaching they need, and which they can find nowhere else. And it may well be, if one may be allowed to speculate on such a thing, that the Holy Spirit led the early Church to adopt the Old Testament writings partly for that reason. What we find from the beginning to the end of the Bible is the account of God's dealings with His people. He is the same God in the Old Testament as in the New; and these Old Testament saints were citizens of the kingdom of God even as we are. We are taken into a kingdom which already contains such people as Abraham, Isaac and Jacob. The mystery that was revealed to the apostles was that the Gentiles should be fellow-heirs and citizens in the kingdom with the Jews.

It is right, therefore, to regard the experiences of these people as being exactly parallel with our own. The fact that they lived in the old dispensation makes no difference. There is something wrong with a Christianity which rejects the Old Testament, or even with a Christianity which imagines that we are essentially different from the Old Testament saints. If any of you are tempted to feel like that, I would invite you to read the Book of Psalms, and then to ask yourself whether you can honestly say from your experience some of the things the Psalmists said. Can you say, "When my father and my mother forsake me, then the Lord will take me up?" Can you say, "As the hart panteth after the water brooks, so panteth my soul after thee, O God?" Read the Psalms and the statements made in them, and I think you will agree that these men were children of God with a great and rich spiritual experience. For this reason, it has been the practice in the Christian Church from the beginning for men and women to come to the Book of Psalms for light, knowledge, and instruction.

The Value of the Psalms

Its special value lies in the fact that *it helps us by putting its teaching chiefly in the form of the recital of experiences.* We have exactly the same teaching in the New Testament, only there it is given in a more didactic fashion. Here it seems to come down to our own ordinary and practical level. Now we are all familiar with the value of this. There are times when the soul is weary, when we feel we are incapable of receiving that more direct instruction; we are so tried, and our minds are so tired, and our hearts may be so bruised, that we somehow cannot make the effort to concentrate upon principles and to look at things objectively. It is at such a time, and particularly at such a time, and in order that they may receive truth in this more personal form, that people who feel that life has dealt cruelly with them have gone—battered and beaten by the waves and billows of life—to the Psalms. They have read the experiences of some of these men, and have found that they, too, have been through something very similar. And somehow that fact, in and of itself, helps and strengthens them. They feel that they are not alone, and that what is happening to them is not unusual. They begin to realize the truth of Paul's comforting words to the Corinthians, "There hath no temptation taken you but such as is common to man" (1 Corinthians 10:13), and that very realization alone enables them to take courage and to be renewed in their faith. The Book of Psalms is of inestimable value in this respect, and we find people turning constantly to it.

There are many features about the Psalms which might detain us. The thing I want to mention especially is the very remarkable honesty with which *the authors do not hesitate to tell the truth about themselves.* We have a great classic example of that here in the seventy-third Psalm. This man admits very freely that as for him his feet were almost gone, his steps had well-nigh slipped. And he goes on to say that he was like a beast before God, so foolish and so ignorant. What honesty! That is the great value of the Psalms. I know of nothing in the spiritual life more discouraging than to meet the kind of person who seems to give the impression that he or she is always walking on the mountain top. That is certainly not true in the Bible. The Bible tells us that these men knew what it was to be cast down, and to be in sore and grievous trouble. Many a saint in his pilgrimage has thanked God for the honesty of the writers of the Psalms. They do not just put up an ideal teaching which was not true in their own lives. Perfectionist teachings are never true. They are not true to the experience of the people who teach them, for we know that they are fallible creatures like the rest of us. They put their teaching of perfection forward theoretically, but it is not true to their experience. Thank God the Psalmists do not do that. They tell us the plain truth about themselves; they tell us the plain truth about what has happened to them.

Now their motive in doing so is not to exhibit themselves. Confession of sin can be a form of exhibitionism. There are some people who are very willing to confess their sins, so long as they can talk about themselves. It is a very subtle danger. The Psalmist does not do that; he tells us the truth about himself because he wants to glorify God. His honesty is dictated by that, for it is as he shows the contrast between himself and God that he ministers to the glory of God.

That is what this man does here. Notice that he starts off with a great triumphant note, "Truly God is good to Israel, even to such as are of a clean heart," as if to say, "Now I am going to tell you a story. I am going to tell you what has happened to me; but the thing I want to leave with you is just this—the goodness of God." This comes out particularly clear if you take another, and probably better, translation, "God is always good to

Israel, even to such as are of a clean heart." God never varies. There is no limitation at all, there are no qualifications. "This is my proposition," says this man, "God is always good to Israel." Most of the Psalms start with some such great burst of praise and of thanksgiving.

Again, as has often been pointed out, the Psalms generally start with a conclusion. That sounds paradoxical, but I am not trying to be paradoxical: it is true. This man had had an experience. He went right through it and reached this point. Now the great thing to him was that he had arrived there. So he starts with the end; and then he proceeds to tell us how he got there. This is a good way of teaching; and it is always the method of the Psalms. The value of the experience is that it is an illustration of this particular truth. It is of no interest in and of itself, and the Psalmist is not interested in it as an experience *qua* experience. But *it is an illustration of this great truth about God,* and therein lies its value.

The great thing is that we should all realize this big point that he is making, namely, *that God is always good to His people,* to such as are of a clean heart. That is the proposition; but the thing that will engage us, as we study this Psalm in particular, is the method, the way, by which this man arrives at that conclusion. What he has to tell us can be summed up like this: He started from this proposition in his religious experience; then he went astray; then he came back again. It is because they analyze such experiences that we find the Psalms to be of such great value. We all know something about that same kind of experience in our own lives. We start in the right place; then something goes wrong, and we seem somehow to be losing everything. The problem is how to get back again. What this man does is to show us how to arrive back at that place where the soul finds her true poise.

This Psalm is only one illustration. You can find many others that do exactly the same thing. Take Psalm 43, for instance, where you find the Psalmist in a similar condition. He addresses himself, and says, "Why art thou cast down, O my soul? and why art thou disquieted within me?" (v. 5). He talks to himself, he addresses his soul. Now that is just what he is doing in Psalm 73, only here it is elaborated and brought before us in a very striking manner.

This man tells us all about a particular experience that he had passed through. He tells us that he was very badly shaken, and that he very nearly fell. What was the cause of his trouble? Simply that he did not quite understand God's way with respect to him. He had become aware of a painful fact. Here he was living a godly life; he was cleansing his heart, he tells us, and washing his hands in innocency. In other words, he was practicing the godly life. He was avoiding sin; he was meditating upon the things of God; he was spending his time in prayer to God; he was in the habit of examining his life, and whenever he found sin he confessed it to God with sorrow, and he sought forgiveness and renewal. The man was devoting himself to a life which would be well-pleasing in God's sight. He kept clear of the world and its polluting effects; he separated himself from evil ways, and gave himself up to the living of this godly life. Yet, although he was doing all this, he was having a great deal of trouble, "all the day long have I been plagued, and chastened every morning." He was having a very hard and difficult time. He does not tell us exactly what was happening; it may have been illness, sickness, trouble in his family. Whatever it was, it was very grievous and hurtful; he was being tried, and tried very sorely. In fact, everything seemed to be going wrong and nothing seemed to be going right.

Now that was bad enough in itself. But that was not the thing that really troubled and distressed him. The real trouble was that when he looked at the ungodly he saw a striking contrast. "These men," he said, "we all know to be ungodly—it is quite clear to everybody that they are ungodly. But they prosper in the world, they increase in riches, there are no bands—no pangs—in their death, but their strength is firm, they are not in trouble as other men." He gives this description of them in their arrogance, their deceitfulness, their blasphemy. He gives us the most perfect picture in all literature of the so-called successful man of the world. He even describes his posture, his arrogant appearance, with his eyes standing out with fatness, and his pride compassing him about as a chain—a necklace. "Violence covers them as a garment," he says, "they have more than heart could wish," "they speak loftily"—what a perfect description it is.

Moreover, not only was it true of people who lived at the time of the Psalmist, but you see the same kind of person today. They make blasphemous statements about God. They say, "How doth God know, and is there knowledge in the most High?" You talk about your God, they say; we don't believe in your God, yet look at us. Nothing goes wrong with us. But you, who are so godly, look at the things that happen to you! Now this was what caused this man his pain and his trouble. He believed God to be holy and righteous and true, One who intervenes on behalf of His people and surrounds them with loving care and wonderful promises. His problem was how to reconcile all this with what was happening to himself, and still more with what was happening to the ungodly.

This Psalm is a classic statement of this particular problem—God's ways with respect to man, and especially God's ways with respect to His own people. That was the thing that perplexed this psalmist as he contrasted his own lot with that of the wicked. And he tells us his reaction to it all.

Perplexity Is Not Surprising

Now let us content ourselves for the moment with drawing some general but very important lessons from all this. The first comment which we must make is that *perplexity in the light of this kind of situation is not surprising*. This, I would say, is a fundamental principle, for we are dealing with the ways of Almighty God, and He has told us so often in His Book, "My thoughts are not your thoughts, neither are your ways my ways" (Isaiah 55:8). Half our trouble arises from the fact that we do not realize that that is the basic position from which we must always start. I think that many of us get into trouble just because we forget that we are really dealing with the mind of God, and that God's mind is not like our mind. We desire everything to be cut and dried and simple, and feel that there should never be any problems or difficulties. But if there is one thing that is taught more clearly than anything else in the Bible, it is that that is never the case in our dealings with God. The ways of God are inscrutable; His mind is infinite and eternal, and His purposes are so great that our sinful minds cannot understand. Therefore, when such a Being is dealing with us, it ought not surprise us if, at times, things take place which are perplexing to us.

We tend to think, of course, that God should be blessing His own children always, and that they should never be chastised. How often have we thought that! Did we not think it during the war? Why is it that God allows certain forms of tyranny to persist, especially those that are absolutely godless? Why does He not wipe them all out, and shower His blessings upon His own people? That is our way of thinking. But it is based on a fallacy. God's mind is eternal, and God's ways are so infinitely above us that we must always start by being prepared not to understand immediately anything He does. If we start with the other supposition, that everything should always be plain and clear, we shall soon find ourselves in the place where this man found himself. It is not surprising that when we look into the mind of the Eternal, there should be times when we are given the impression that things are working out in a manner exactly opposite to what we think they ought to be.

Perplexity Is Not Sinful

Let me now put a second proposition. Perplexity in this matter is not only surprising; I want to emphasize that *to be perplexed is not sinful either.* There, again, is something that is very comforting. There are those who give the impression that they think the ways of God are always perfectly plain and clear; they always seem to be able to reason thus, and the sky to them is always bright and shining, and they themselves are always perfectly happy. Well, all I can say is that they are absolutely superior to the apostle Paul, for he tells us, in 2 Corinthians 4, that he was "perplexed, but not in despair." Ah yes, it is wrong to be in a state of despair; but it is not wrong to be perplexed. Let us draw this clear distinction; the mere fact that you may be perplexed about something that is happening at the present time does not mean that you are guilty of sin. You are in God's hand, and yet something unpleasant is happening to you, and you say: I do not understand. There is nothing wrong with that—"perplexed, but not in despair." The perplexity in and of itself is not sinful, for our minds are not only finite, they are also weakened by sin. We do not see things clearly; we do not know what is best for us; we cannot take the long view; so it is very natural that we should be perplexed.

Perplexity Opens the Door to Temptation

Now although that is not sinful as far as it goes, we must hurry on to say that *to be perplexed always opens the door to temptation.* That is the real message of this Psalm. It is all right up to a point, but as soon as you get into this state of being perplexed, and you can stop and dwell on it for a moment, at that moment temptation is at the door. It is ready to enter in, and before you know what has happened it will have entered in. And that is what had happened to this man.

That brings us to what the Psalmist tells us about the *character of temptation and how important it is to recognize this.* Temptation can be so powerful that not only does it shake the greatest and strongest saint; it does, indeed, get him down. "As for me," says this man of God, "as for me, my feet were almost gone; my steps had well nigh slipped."

"But that was in the Old Testament," you say, "and the Holy Spirit had not come then as He has come now. We are in the Christian position whereas this saint of God was not." All right, if you like you may have it in the words of the apostle Paul, "Wherefore let him that thinketh he standeth take heed lest he fall!" Paul, in explaining the Christian position to the Corinthians

(1 Corinthians 10), goes back for an illustration to the Old Testament; and lest some of those superior people in Corinth might say, We have received the Holy Spirit, we are not like that, he says, "Let him that thinketh he standeth take heed lest he fall" (1 Corinthians 10:12). The man who has not yet discovered the power of temptation is the veriest tyro in spiritual matters. Temptations can come with varying degrees of power and force. The Bible teaches that it comes sometimes to the most spiritual as a veritable hurricane sweeping all before it, with such terrific might that even a man of God is almost overwhelmed. Such is the power of temptation! But let me use again the words of the apostle: "Take unto you the whole armor of God" (Ephesians 6:13). For you need it all. If you are to stand in the evil day you must be completely clothed with the whole armor of God. The might of the enemy against us is second only to the power of God. He is more powerful than any man who has ever lived; and the saints of the Old Testament went down before him. He tempted and tried the Lord Jesus Christ to the ultimate limit. Our Lord defeated him, but He alone has succeeded of all ever born of woman. Go back and read this Psalm again and you will see that temptation came when this man was least expecting it. It came in as the result of what was happening to him, it came through the door that was opened by the trouble he was experiencing, and by the contrast between that and the successful, apparently happy life of the ungodly.

The next point to note about temptation concerns its blinding effect. There is nothing more strange about temptation than the way in which, under its influence and power, we are made to do things that in our normal condition would be quite unthinkable to us. The Psalmist puts it like this—and notice that his wording is almost sarcasm at his own expense. Look at the third verse, "For I was envious at the foolish." He was envious of the arrogant. "You know," he seems to say, "I hardly like to put it on paper, I am so heartily ashamed of it. But I have to confess that there was a moment when I, who have been so blessed of God, was envious of those ungodly people." Only the blinding effect of temptation can explain that. It comes with such force that we are knocked off our balance, and are no longer able to think clearly.

Now there is nothing of more vital importance in this spiritual warfare than for us to realize that we are confronted by a power like that, and that therefore, we cannot afford to relax for one moment. The thing is so powerful that it makes us see only what it wants us to see, and we forget everything else. This is the blinding effect of temptation!

Again, we must not forget the subtlety of Satan. He comes as a would-be friend. He had obviously come to the Psalmist like that. He said, "Don't you think you are cleansing your heart in vain, and washing your hands in innocency?" As the well-known hymn puts it so perfectly:

> Always fast and vigil?
> Always watch and prayer?

"That is what you seem to be doing," says the devil. "You seem to be spending your time in self-denial and prayers. There is something wrong with this outlook of yours. You believe the gospel; but look at what is happening to you! Why are you having this hard time? Why is a God of love dealing with you in this manner? Is that the Christian life you are advocating? My friend," he says, "you are making a mistake; you are doing yourself grievous damage and harm; you are not fair to yourself." Oh, the terrible subtlety of it all.

Again there is *the apparent logic of the case temptation presents.* When it comes thus with its blinding effect it really does seem to be quite innocent and reasonable. "After all," it makes the Psalmist say, "I am living a godly life, and this is what happens to me. Those other men are blaspheming God, and with 'lofty' utterances are saying things which should never be thought, let alone said. Yet they are very propserous; their children are all doing well; they have more than the heart could wish. Meanwhile I am suffering the exact opposite. There is only one conclusion to draw."

Looking at it from the natural human point of view, the case seems to be unanswerable. That is always a characteristic of temptation. No man would ever fall to temptation if it were not. Its plausibility, its power, its strength, its logical and apparently unanswerable case. You know that I am not speaking theoretically. We all know something of this; if we do not, we are not Christian. This is the kind of thing to which God's people are subjected. Because they are God's people the devil makes a special target of them and seizes every opportunity to get them down.

At this point I would stress that *to be tempted in that way is not sin.* We must be clear about this. That such thoughts are put to us, and insinuated into our minds, does not mean that we are guilty of sin. Here again is something which is of fundamental importance in the whole matter of spiritual warfare. We must learn to draw a distinction between being tempted and sinning. You cannot control the thoughts that are put into your mind by the devil. He puts them there. Paul talks of "the fiery darts of the wicked one." Now that is what had been happening to the Psalmist. The devil had been hurling them at him, but the mere fact that they had been coming into his mind does not mean that he was guilty of sin. The Lord Jesus Christ Himself was tempted. The devil put thoughts into His mind. But He did not sin, because He rejected them. Thoughts will come to you and the devil may try to press you to think that because thoughts have entered your mind you have sinned. But they are not your thoughts, they are the devil's—he put them there. It was the quaint Cornishman, Billy Bray, who put this in his own original manner when he said, "You cannot prevent the crow from flying over your head, but you can prevent him from making a nest in your hair!" So I say that we cannot prevent thoughts being insinuated into our mind; but the question is what do we do with them? We talk about thoughts "passing through" the mind, and so long as they do this, they are not sin. But if we welcome them and agree with them then they become sin. I emphasize this because I have often had to deal with people who are in great distress because unworthy thoughts have come to them. But what I say to them is this, "Listen to what you are telling me. You say that the thovght 'has come to you.' Well, if that is true you are not guilty of sin. You do not say, 'I have thought'; you say, 'the thought came.' That is right. The thought came to you, and it came from the devil, and the fact that the thought did come from the devil means that you are not of necessity guilty of sin." Temptation, in and of itself, is not sin.

That brings us to the last and very vital point. It is that *we should know how to deal with temptation when it comes,* and we should know how to handle it. Indeed, in one sense the writer's whole purpose is just to tell us this. There is only one way in which we can be quite sure that we have dealt with temptation in the right way, and that is that we arrive at the right ultimate conclusion. I started with that and I end with it. The great message of this Psalm is, that if you and I know what to do with temptation we can turn it into a great source of victory. We can end, when we have been through a process like this, in a stronger position than we were in at the beginning. We may have been in a situation where our "steps had well nigh slipped." That does not matter so long as, at the end, we arrive on that great high plateau where we stand face to face with God with an assurance we have not had before. We can make use of the devil and all his assaults, but we have to learn how to handle him. We can turn all this into a great spiritual victory, so that we can say, "Well, having been through it all, I have now been given to see that God is always good. I was tempted to think there were times when He was not; I see now that that was wrong. God is always good in all circumstances, in all ways, at all times—no matter what may happen to me, or to anybody else." "I have arrived," says the Psalmist, "at the conclusion that 'God is always good to Israel.' "

Are we all ready to say that? Some of you may be passing through this kind of experience at this moment. Things may be going wrong with you, and you may be having a hard time. Blow upon blow may be descending upon you. You have been living the Christian life, reading your Bible, working for God, and yet the blows have come, one on top of another. Everything seems to be going wrong; you have been plagued "all the day long," and "chastened every morning." One trouble follows hard after another. Now the one simple question I want to ask is this. Are you able to say in the face of it all, "God is always good?" Yes, even in the face of what is happening to you, and even as you see the wicked flourish. In spite of the cruelty of an enemy or the treachery of a friend, in spite of all that is happening to you, can you say, "God is always good; there is no exception; there is no qualification?" Can you say that? Because if you cannot, then you are guilty of sin. You may have been tempted to doubt. That is to be expected; that is not sin. The question is, Were you able to deal with the temptation? Were you able to thrust it back, and to put it out of your mind? Were you able to say, "God is always good," without any reservation at all? Are you able to say, "All things work together for good," without any hesitation? That is the test. But let me remind you that while the Psalmist says, "God is always good to Israel," he is careful to add, "Even to such as are of a clean heart."

Now we must be careful. We must be fair to ourselves; we must be fair to God. The promises of God are great, and all-inclusive. But they always have this condition, "to them that are of a clean heart." In other words, if you and I are sinning against God, then God will have to deal with us, and it is going to be painful. But even when God chastises us He is still good to us. It is because He is good to us that He chastises us. If we do not experience chastisement, then we are "bastards," as the author of the Epistle to the Hebrews reminds us. But, let us remember, if we want to see this clearly we must be of a clean heart. We must have "truth in [our] inward parts," and there must be no hidden sin, because "if I regard iniquity in my heart, the Lord will not hear me" (Psalm 66:18). If I am not true and straight with God I have no right to appropriate any of the promises. If, on the other hand, it is my one desire to be right with Him, then I can say that absolutely "God is always good to Israel."

I sometimes think that the very essence of the whole Christian position, and the secret of a successful spiritual life, is just to realize two things. They are in these first two verses, "Truly God is good to Israel, even to such as are of a clean heart. But as for me, my feet were almost gone; my steps had well nigh slipped." In other words, I must have complete, absolute confidence in God, and no confidence in myself. As long as you and I are in the position in which we "worship God in the Spirit, and rejoice in Christ Jesus, and have no confidence in the flesh" all is well with us. That is to be truly Christian—on the one hand utter absolute confidence in God, and on the other no confidence in myself and what I may do. If I take that view of myself, it means that I shall always be looking to God. And in that position I shall never fail.

May God grant us grace to apply some of these simple principles to ourselves and, as we do so, let us remember that we have the greatest and the grandest illustration of it all in our blessed Lord Himself. I see Him in the Garden of Gethsemane, the very Son of God, and I hear Him uttering these words, "Father, if it be possible." There was perplexity. He asked, Is there no other way, is this the only way whereby mankind can be saved? The thought of the sin of the world coming between Him and His Father perplexed Him. But He humbled Himself. The perplexity did not cause Him to fall, He just committed Himself to God saying in effect, "Thy ways are always right, Thou art always good, and as for what Thou art going to do to Me I know it is because Thou art good. Not My will, but Thine, be done."

NOTES

Hopeful's Text

Frank W. Boreham (1871-1959) was the last student personally chosen by Charles H. Spurgeon to enter the Pastor's College in London. He ministered effectively in New Zealand, Australia, and Tasmania; and then resigned from pastoral ministry to minister around the world to appreciative congregations. He is best known as a writer of delightful essays and has more than fifty books to his credit. His sermon series "Texts That Made History" is published in five volumes and has become a homiletical classic. This sermon is taken from *A Faggot of Torches,* Volume 3.

Frank W. Boreham

5

HOPEFUL'S* TEXT

I will stand upon my watch, and set myself upon the tower, and will watch to see what he will say unto me, and what I shall answer when I am reproved. And the Lord answered me, and said, Write the vision, and make it plain upon tables, that he may run that readeth it. For the vision is yet for an appointed time, but at the end it shall speak, and not lie; though it tarry, wait for it, because it will surely come, it will not tarry (Habakkuk 2:1-3).

WHEN THE PILGRIMS were taking a reluctant farewell of the Delectable Mountains, the shepherds who had so hospitably entertained them warned them concerning the Enchanted Ground that lay but a short distance ahead of them. "Beware," they said, "of sleeping there; for he who sleeps on the Enchanted Ground will never wake again!" When, however, the pilgrims reached the treacherous and seductive spot, they were so drowsy that they could scarcely keep their eyelids apart. Hopeful pleaded for one little nap, but Christian would not hear of it. And, to put the matter beyond the pale of possibility, he made his companion talk. "Tell me," he said, "by what means you were led to go on pilgrimage." And, when Hopeful unfolded his story, it turned, as so many stories do, upon a text. He told how, in his anxiety and concern, he had opened his mind to Faithful. For Hopeful was a citizen of Vanity Fair and it was at Vanity Fair that Faithful had suffered martyrdom. And Faithful, he explained, had urged him to look in his distress to Jesus and to cry to God for mercy.

"And," asked Christian, partly because he was interested and partly because he was anxious to keep his companion talking, "did you do as you were bidden?"

"Yes," replied Hopeful, "over and over and over again."

---

*Taken from the character of *Pilgrim's Progress* by John Bunyan.

"And did the Father reveal the Son to you?"

"Not at first, nor second, nor third, nor fourth, nor fifth, no, nor at the sixth time either."

"What did you do then?"

"What! Why, I could not tell what to do."

"Had you no thoughts of leaving off praying?"

"Yes, an hundred times, twice told."

"And what was the reason you did not?"

"This word from Habakkuk came into my mind: 'I will stand upon my watch, and set myself upon the tower, and will watch to see what He will say unto me. . . . Though the vision tarry, wait for it; because it will surely come, it will not tarry.' So I continued praying until the Father showed me the Son."

"And how," asked Christian, determined that the conversation, once started, should know no lull, "how was He revealed to you?"

"One day," replied Hopeful, "I was very sad; sadder, I think, than I had ever been before; and this sadness was through a fresh sight of the greatness and vileness of my sins. And as I was then looking for nothing but the everlasting damnation of my soul, suddenly, as I thought, I saw the Lord Jesus look down from heaven upon me, saying: 'Believe on the Lord Jesus Christ and thou shalt be saved.' 'But,' I replied, 'I am a great, a very great sinner, O Lord!' and He answered: 'My grace is sufficient for thee!' And now was my heart full of joy, mine eyes full of tears and mine affections running over!"

And so Hopeful told how, by means of the text, he was led into the faith that persevered and overcame; and, by the mere telling of the story, he and his fellow pilgrim were saved from sleeping on the Enchanted Ground.

Habakkuk is the skeptic of the Old Testament as Thomas is the skeptic of the New. He stands in a maze of bewilderment. He cannot reconcile fact and faith. If God is in His heaven, why are things as they are? The earth, he cries, is deluged in wickedness; the innocent are like fish caught in the tyrant's drag-net; right is on the scaffold and wrong is on the throne! It is the old, old mystery: the problem that has shaken the faith alike of the simpleton and of the sage. It has sent men like Goethe and women like George Eliot out into the bleak wilderness of doubt and uncertainty; it has puzzled minds not given to suspicion and distrust.

"God lets them!" cried poor George Harris, in *Uncle Tom's Cabin,* as he bitterly enumerated the atrocities committed by the pitiless slave-holders. He writhes at the thought that, do what he may, he is still a slave and that his wife and child may be sold away from him at any moment. "They buy and sell us, and make trade of our heart's blood and groans and tears, and God lets them, He does; *God lets them!*"

And Dickens has shown how poor demented Barnaby Rudge was baffled by the same acute perplexity. Gabriel Vardon comes upon Barnaby, the lunatic lad, at dead of night, bending over the prostrate, bleeding form of a man who has fallen a victim to highway robbery. "See," says Barnaby, "when I talk of eyes the stars come out! Whose eyes are they? If they are angels' eyes, why do they look down here and see good men hurt, and only wink and sparkle all the night?"

That is the question—Barnaby's question; George Harris's question; my question; everybody's question! The distinction of Habakkuk lies not in the question, but in the answer. He simply declines to answer it. "I do not understand," he says, "so I will keep an open mind. I will stand; I will watch; I will tarry; I will wait with patience till the explanation comes!" In his *Foundations of Zoology,* Professor W. K. Brooks declares that the hardest of intellectual virtues is philosophic doubt. "Suspended judgment," he adds, "is the supreme triumph of intellectual discipline." It is the glory of Habakkuk that he develops that hardest of all the intellectual virtues and achieves that "supreme triumph of intellectual discipline." Anybody, seeing difficulties in belief, can rush to unbelief; anybody, finding faith in seeming conflict with the facts of life, can abandon faith. Habakkuk declines to do anything of the kind. He knows a more excellent way.

"I will stand upon my watch," he says, "and set myself

upon the tower, and will watch to see what He will say unto me. . . . Though the vision tarry, wait for it; because it will surely come, it will not tarry."

The Jealousy of a Staggering Faith

Habakkuk is the supreme example of the *jealousy of a staggering faith.* "To the watch-tower!" he says; he realizes that he has something to guard. "To the ramparts!" he says; he realizes that he has something to hold.

> On my watch-tower will I stand,
> And take up my post on the rampart;
> I will watch to see what He says to me
> And what answer I get back to my plea.

The translation is that of Principal Sir George Adam Smith. "Through these words," says that greatest of our Hebrew scholars, "through these choice words there breathes a noble sense of responsibility. The prophet feels that he has a post to hold, a rampart to guard. He knows the heritage of truth, won by the great minds of the past; and, in a world seething with disorder, he will take his stand upon *that,* and see what more his God will send him." A merchant who, today, finds things going hardly with him, clings all the more tenaciously to the treasure which he has accumulated in more prosperous years. Like the bees that, in the winter, live on the honey that they have stored in the summer, the soul must learn to sing in days of gloom the songs that she learned in days of gladness.

I once spent the closing days of the old year at the homestead of Andrew Wallace, at Twilight Glen, near Mosgiel. Andrew was a sturdy young Scotsman who had been only ten or twelve years out from Ayrshire. He had married a New Zealand girl and they had two children, Ian and Pearl. I found the youngsters great fun. One evening they were showing me the presents that Santa Claus had brought them. The assortment included a picture-puzzle. We all set to work fitting together the fantastically shaped fragments; but as the task approached completion it became evident that some of the pieces were missing.

"Oh," exclaimed Pearl, in impatient disgust, "we must throw them all away; they're no good now!"

"Oh, yes they are," replied her wiser brother, "the other pieces may turn up some day; we'll keep these in the cupboard 'til they do!"

That is Habakkuk's argument exactly. When the soul is confronted by a perplexity that is too baffling for her, she is tempted to throw everything to the winds. But let her pause and think! Shall she fling away the answers to ninety-nine questions simply because there is one problem that she cannot satisfactorily solve? Shall I hurl into the void my hoard of golden yesterdays simply because I cannot understand God's inscrutable tomorrows?

"To the watch-tower!" cries the prophet.

"To the ramparts!" says Hopeful's text.

When, at some one point, faith is assailed, the time has come to guard her priceless hoard.

The Vigilance of a Staggering Faith

Habakkuk is the supreme example of the *vigilance of a staggering faith.* "I will watch," he says; "I will watch to see what He says to me!" Habakkuk felt, as Christian and Hopeful did, that it would never do to go to sleep. When the problems of life prove baffling, faith must remain open-eyed, quickwitted, and alert. The explanation of the mystery may arrive at any moment, and it may emerge from the most unlikely quarter. Under such circumstances therefore, how can I consent to fold my hands or close my eyes or compose my mind to slumber? He who sleeps on the Enchanted Ground, the Shepherds said, will never wake again. He who complacently settles down in the midst of his doubts can never expect to again behold the beatific vision. "I will watch!" said the prophet, "I will watch!"

In the course of his Presidential Address at the annual meeting of the British Association, Sir Michael Foster outlines the three qualifications that represent the essentials of a distinctively scientific spirit. The first is *absolute truthfulness;* the third is *moral courage;* and the second is "*alertness of mind;* a mind ever on the watch; ready at once to lay hold of Nature's hint, however small; and to listen to Nature's whisper, however low."

Habakkuk's attitude could not have been more felicitously expressed. "I cannot solve the problem," he says, "but I will keep my eyes wide open. I cannot read the riddle; but I will scan the whole horizon in search of the answer. I will watch, as a sentry watches, for any movement, any sign, any shadow that may denote the approach of the solution. Remembering that those who sleep among their doubts sleep to wake no more, I will give myself no rest nor slumber. My mind shall be vigilant, watchful, alert; ready to lay hold on any hint, however small, and to listen to any whisper, however low!" Such wakeful eyes are seldom cheated of the vision for which they so tirelessly and hungrily watch.

The Patience of a Staggering Faith

Habakkuk is the supreme example of the *patience of a staggering faith.* "Though it tarry," he says, "I will wait for it." It often tarries. It did in Hopeful's case.

"And did the Father reveal the Son to you?"

"No, not at the first, nor second, nor third, nor fourth, nor the fifth, no, nor at the sixth time either."

"Had you no thoughts of leaving off praying?"

"Yes, a hundred times twice told."

The vision tarried; but Hopeful remembered Habakkuk. "Though it tarry, wait for it." And, waiting, he soon found his heart full of joy, his eyes full of tears and his affections running over.

Patience was ever the golden key that opened the gates of vision. Richard Jefferies used to talk to his friends of the wonders he had seen in the woods—the pheasant down in the fern, the hare out in the open, the squirrel perched in the pine-trees, and the woodpecker up in the copse. As soon as they were at liberty to do so, his delighted hearers would set off to see these pretty creatures for themselves. But they invariably returned disappointed from their quest.

"We went to the fern and saw no pheasants," they

would complain; "there was no squirrel in the pine-tree, no hare in the stubble, and no woodpecker in the copse! How is it that *you* saw these things and *we* didn't?"

"Because," Jefferies would reply with a chuckle, "because I don't mind crouching for two hours in a wet ditch!"

Darwin watched his earthworms for twenty-nine years to learn the secrets with which he afterwards astonished the world. M. Fabre, "the Virgil of the Insects," was said to have been "an incomparable observer." And, when he died, the *Times* remarked that, "in this age of haste, his example was a valuable and lofty lesson. For seventy years he had bent over the same task, and he seemed to be telling those who were in a hurry to achieve a fleeting reputation that, in order to lay the foundations of a solid and durable monument, the whole life of a man is not too much." The vision tarried, but he waited, and, by waiting, came to his own.

"Wait and see!" we say. To wait is to see. When John Linnell, the famous artist, was painting the picture that he regarded as his masterpiece, some of his friends displayed a tiresome anxiety to view it before it was ready. Linnell was particularly sensitive on the point, and, fearing that, in his absence, some curious visitor might invade the sanctity of his studio, he kept the easel veiled. And across the veil he threw a streamer bearing the inscription "Wait and you shall see!"

That inscription across the veiled picture is the inscription that is written across all veiled things. Our mysteries yield to patience, and to patience only. Waiting is the secret of seeing. The vision that will banish my perplexities may tarry, says the prophet; but, though it tarry, I will wait for it.

The Witness of a Staggering Faith

Habakkuk is the supreme example of the *witness of a staggering faith.* The moment that the vision comes, he is prepared to pass it on. "Write the vision and make it plain upon tables that he may run that readeth it." He stands, like a telegraphist at the receiver, interpreting the message, and simultaneously, preparing to dispatch it. The moment that his own perplexities are scattered, the prophet will do his best to dispel the cheerless gloom of every other doubter.

"This was a revelation to your soul, indeed," said Christian, after listening to Hopeful's affecting recital. "Tell me particularly what effect this had upon your spirit!"

"It made me love a holy life and long to do something for the honor and glory of the Lord Jesus. Yea, I thought that, had I now a thousand gallons of blood in my body, I could spill it all for the sake of the Lord Jesus."

Every man who, after long waiting and eager watching, has at last caught the vision that has filled his life with splendor, will sympathize and understand.

NOTES

Justification by Faith

Martin Luther (1483-1546) is Germany's best-known preacher and religious leader. He was trained as an Augustinian monk, and lectured on the Bible at the University of Wittenberg. Never satisfied with his spiritual experience, Luther found peace through the study of Paul's epistles, when he discovered salvation by grace alone through faith in Jesus Christ. His opposition to the scandals relating to the sale of indulgences eventually led to the Reformation and the founding of the Lutheran Church. He was a conscientious preacher who sought to make the Bible meaningful to the common people. He wrote more than 400 works, from pamphlets to books as well as 125 hymns. This sermon is reprinted from *The Precious and Sacred Writings of Martin Luther,* vol. IV, edited by John Nicholas Lenker and published in 1904 by Lutherans in All Lands Co.

Martin Luther

6

JUSTIFICATION BY FAITH

> And he said unto his disciples, There was a certain rich man, which had a steward; and the same was accused unto him that he had wasted his goods. And he called him, and said unto him, How is it that I hear this of thee? give an account of thy stewardship; for thou mayest be no longer steward. Then the steward said within himself, What shall I do? for my lord taketh away from me the stewardship: I cannot dig; to beg I am ashamed. I am resolved what to do, that, when I am put out of the stewardship, they may receive me into their houses. So he called every one of his lord's debtors unto him, and said unto the first, How much owest thou unto my Lord? And he said, An hundred measures of oil. And he said unto him, Take thy bill, and sit down quickly, and write fifty. Then said he to another, And how much owest thou? And he said, An hundred measures of wheat. And he said unto him, Take thy bill, and write fourscore. And the lord commended the unjust steward, because he had done wisely: for the children of this world are in their generation wiser than the children of light. And I say unto you, Make to yourselves friends of the mammon of unrighteousness; that, when ye fail, they may receive you into everlasting habitations (Luke 16:1-9).

ALTHOUGH IN MY little book, *Christian Liberty and Good Works,* I have taught very extensively how faith alone without work justifies, and good works are done first after we believe, that it seems I should henceforth politely keep quiet, and give every mind and heart an opportunity to understand and explain all the Gospel lessons for themselves; yet I perceive that the Gospel abides and prospers only among the few; the people are constantly dispirited and terrified by the passages that treat of good works; so that I see plainly how necessary it is, either to write Postils on each Gospel lesson, or to appoint sensible ministers in all places who can orally explain and teach these things.

If this Gospel be considered without the Spirit, by mere reason, it truly favors the priests and monks, and could be made to serve covetousness and to establish one's own works. For when Christ says: "Make to yourselves friends by means of the mammon of unrighteousness; that, when it shall fail, they may receive you into everlasting habitations" (Luke 6:9); they force from it three points against our doctrine of faith, namely: first, against that we teach faith alone justifies and saves from sin; second, that all good works ought to be gratuitously done to our neighbors out of free love; third, that we should not put any value in the merits of saints or of others.

Against our first proposition they claim that the Lord says here: "Make to yourselves friends by means of the mammon of unrighteousness," just as though works should make us friends, who previously were enemies. Against the second, is what He says: "That they may receive you into the everlasting habitations;" just as though we should do the work for our own sakes and benefit. And against the third they quote: "The friends may receive us into the everlasting habitation;" just as though we should serve the saints and trust in them to get to heaven. For the sake of the weak we reply to these:

Faith Alone Makes Us Good, and Friends of God

The foundation must be maintained without wavering, that faith without any works, without any merit, reconciles man to God and makes him good, as Paul says to the Romans: "But now the righteousness of God without the law is manifested, being witnessed by the law and the prophets; even the righteousness of God which is by faith of Jesus Christ . . . unto all them that believe" (Romans 3:21-22). Paul at another place says: "To Abraham, his faith was reckoned for righteousness;" so also with us. Again: "Therefore being justified by faith, we have peace with God through our Lord Jesus Christ" (Romans 5:1). Again: "For with the heart man believeth unto righteousness; and with the mouth confession is made unto salvation" (Romans 10:10). These, and many similar passages, we must firmly hold and trust in them immovably, so that to faith alone without any assistance of works, is attributed the forgiveness of sins and our justification.

Take for an illustration the parable of Christ: "Even so every good tree bringeth forth good fruit; but a corrupt tree bringeth forth evil fruit" (Matthew 7:17). Here you see that the fruit does not make the tree good, but without any fruit and before any fruit the tree must be first good, or made good, before it can bear good fruit. As He also says: "Either make the tree good, and its fruit good; or else make the tree corrupt, and its fruit corrupt: for the tree is known by its fruit. Ye generation of vipers, how can ye, being evil, speak good things?" (Matthew 12:33-34). Thus it is the naked truth, that a man must be good without good works, and before he does any good works. And it is clear how impossible it is that a man should become good by works, when he is not good before he does the good works. For Christ stands firm when He says: "How can ye, being evil, speak good things?" And hence follows: How can ye, being evil, do good things?

Therefore, the powerful conclusion follows. There must be something far greater and more precious than all good works, by which a man becomes pious and good, before he does good; just as he must first be in bodily health before he can labor and do hard work. This great and precious something is the noble Word of God, which offers us in the Gospel the grace of God in Christ. He who hears and believes this, thereby becomes good and righteous. Wherefore it is called the Word of Life, a Word of Grace, a Word of Forgiveness. But he who neither hears nor believes it, can in no way become good. For Peter says in Acts 15:9. "And he made no distinction between us and them, cleansing their hearts by faith." For as the Word is, so will the heart be, which believes and cleaves firmly to it. The Word is a living, righteous, truthful, pure and good Word, so also the heart which cleaves to it, must be living, just, truthful, pure and good.

What now shall we say of those passages which so strongly insist on good works, as when the Lord says in Luke 16:9: "Make to yourselves friends by means of the mammon of unrighteousness?" And in Matthew 25:42: "For I was hungry, and ye did not give me to eat." And many other similar passages, which sound altogether as though we had become good by works. We answer thus:

There are some who hear and read the Gospel and what is said by faith, and immediately conclude that they have formed a correct notion of what faith is. They do not think that faith is anything else than something which is altogether in their own power to have or not to have, as any other natural human work. Hence, when in their hearts they begin to think and say: "Verily, the doctrine is right, and I believe it is true," then they immediately think faith is present. But as soon as they see and feel in themselves and others that no change has taken place, and that the works do not follow and they remain as before in their old ways, then they conclude that faith is not sufficient, that they must have something more and greater than faith.

Behold, how they then seize the opportunity, and cry and say, Oh, faith alone does not do it. Why? Oh, because there are so many who believe, and are no better than before, and have not changed their minds at all. Such people are those whom Jude in his Epistle calls dreamers who deceive themselves with their own dreams. For what are such thoughts of theirs which they call faith, but a dream, a dark shadow of faith, which they themselves have created in their own thoughts, by their own strength without the grace of God? They become worse than they were before. For it happens with them as the Lord says: "Neither do men put new wine into old wine-skins; else the skins burst, and the wine is spilled" (Matthew 9:17). That is, they hear God's Word and do not lay hold of it; therefore, they burst and become worse.

But true faith, of which we speak, cannot be manufactured by our own thoughts, for it is solely a work of God in us, without any assistance on our part. As Paul says to the Romans, it is God's gift and grace, obtained by one man, Christ. Therefore, faith is something very powerful, active, restless, effective, which at once renews a person and again regenerates him, and leads him altogether into a new manner and character of life, so that it is impossible not to do good without ceasing.

For just as natural as it is for the tree to produce fruit, so natural is it for faith to produce good works. And just as it is quite unnecessary to command the tree to bear fruit, so there is no command given to the believer, as Paul says, nor is urging necessary for him to do good, for he does it of himself, freely and unconstrained; just as he of himself without command sleeps, eats, drinks, puts on his clothes, hears, speaks, goes and comes.

Whoever has not this faith talks but vainly about faith and works, and does not himself know what he says or whither it tends. He has not received it. He juggles with lies and applies the Scriptures where they speak of faith and works to his own dreams and false thoughts, which is purely a human work, whereas the Scriptures attribute both faith and good works not to ourselves, but to God alone.

Is not this a perverted and blind people? They teach we cannot do a good deed of ourselves, and then in their presumption go to work and arrogate to themselves the highest of all the works of God, namely faith, to manufacture it themselves out of their own perverted thoughts. Wherefore I have said that we should despair of ourselves and pray to God for faith as the apostles did in Luke 17:5. When we have faith, we need nothing more; for it brings with it the Holy Spirit, who then teaches us not only all things, but also establishes us firmly in it, and leads us through death and hell to heaven.

Now observe, we have given these answers, that the Scriptures have such passages concerning works, on account of such dreamers and self-invented faith; not that man should become good by works, but that man should thereby prove and see the difference between false and true faith. For wherever faith is right it does good. If it does no good, it is then certainly a dream and a false idea of faith. So, just as the fruit on the tree does not make the tree good, but nevertheless outwardly proves and testifies that the tree is good, as Christ says, "By their fruits ye shall know them." Thus we should also learn to know faith by its fruits.

From this you see, there is a great difference between being good, and to be known as good; or to become good and to prove and show that you are good. Faith makes good, but works prove the faith and goodness to be right. Thus the Scriptures speak plainly, which prevails among the common people, as when a father says unto his son, "Go and be merciful, good and friendly to this or to that poor person." He does not command him to be merciful, good and friendly, but because he is already good and merciful, he requires that he should also show and prove it outwardly toward the poor by his act, in order that the goodness which he has in himself may also be known to others and be helpful to them.

You should explain all passages of Scripture referring to works, that God thereby desires to let the goodness received in faith express and prove itself, and become a benefit to others, so that false faith may become known and rooted out of the heart. God gives no one His grace that it may remain inactive and accomplish nothing good, but in order that it may bear interest, and by being publicly known and proved externally, draw every one to God, as Christ says: "Let your light so shine before men, that they may see your good works, and glorify your Father which is in heaven" (Matthew 5:16). Otherwise it would be but a buried treasure and a hidden light. But what profit is there in either? Yea, goodness does not only thereby become known to others, but we ourselves also become certain that we are honest, as Peter says: "Wherefore, brethren, give the more diligence to make your calling and election sure" (2 Peter 1:10). Where works do not follow, a man cannot know whether his faith is right; yea, he may be certain that his faith is a dream, and not right as it should be. Thus Abraham became certain of his faith, and that he feared God, when he offered up his son. As God by the angel said to Abraham: "Now I know, that is, it is manifest, that thou fearest God, seeing thou hast not withheld thy son, thine only son, from me" (Genesis 22:12).

Then abide by the truth, that man is internally, in spirit before God, justified by faith alone without works, but externally and publicly before men and himself, he is justified by works, that he is at heart an honest believer and pious. The one you may call a public or outward justification, the other an inner justification, yet in the sense that the public or external justification is only the fruit, the result and proof of the justification in the heart, that a man does not become just thereby before God, but must previously be just before Him. So you may call the fruit of the tree the public or outward good of the tree, which is only the result and proof of its inner and natural goodness.

This is what James means when he says in his Epistle: "Faith without works is dead" (2:26). That is, as the works do not follow, it is a sure sign that there is no faith there; but only an empty thought and dream, which they falsely call faith. Now we understand the words of Christ: "Make to yourselves friends by means of the mammon of unrighteousness." That is, prove your faith publicly by your outward gifts, by which you win friends, that the poor may be witnesses of your public work, that your faith is genuine. For mere external giving in itself can never make friends, unless it proceed from faith, as Christ rejects the alms of the Pharisees that they thereby make no friends because their heart is false. Thus no heart can ever be right without faith, so that even nature forces the confession that no work makes one good, but that the heart must first be good and upright.

All Works Must Be Done Freely and Gratuitously, Without Seeking Gain By Them

Christ means this when He says: "Freely ye have received, freely give" (Matthew 10:8). For just as Christ with all His works did not merit heaven for Himself, because it was His before; but He served us thereby, not regarding or seeking His own, but these two things, namely, our benefit and the glory of God His Father; so also should we never seek our own in our good works, either temporal or eternal, but glorify God by freely and gratuitously doing good to our neighbor. This Paul teaches the Philippians, "Let this mind be in you, which was also in Christ Jesus: who, being in the form of God thought it not robbery to be equal with God: but made himself of no reputation, and took upon him the form of a servant, and was made in the likeness of men; and being found in fashion as a man, he humbled himself, and became obedient unto death, even the death of the cross" (Philippians 2:5-8). That is, for Himself He had enough, since in Him dwelt all the fulness of the Godhead bodily; and yet He served us and became our servant.

And this is the cause; for since faith justifies and destroys sin before God, so it gives life and salvation. And now it would be a lasting shame and disgrace, and injurious to faith, if any one by his life and works would desire to obtain what faith already possesses and brings with it. Just as Christ would have only disgraced Himself had He done good in order to become the Son of God and Lord over all things, which He already was before. So faith makes us God's children, as John 9:12 says: "But as many as received Him, to them gave He the right to become the children of God, even to them that believe on His name." But if they are children, then they are heirs, as Paul says, "How then can we do anything to obtain the inheritance, which we already have by faith?"

But what shall we say of passages that insist on a good life for the sake of an external reward as this one does: "Make to yourselves friends by means of the mammon of unrighteousness"? And in Matthew 19:17: "But if thou wouldst enter into life, keep the commandments." "Lay up for yourselves treasures in heaven" (6:20). We will say this; that those who do not know faith, only speak and think of the reward, as of works. They think that the same rule obtains here as in human affairs, that they must earn the Kingdom of heaven by their works. These, too, are dreams and false views, of which Malachi speaks: "Oh, that there were one among you that would shut the doors, that ye might not kindle fire on mine altar in vain!" (Malachi 1:10). They are slaves and greedy self-enjoying hirelings and day laborers, who receive their reward here on earth, like the Pharisees with their praying and fasting, as Christ says.

However, in regard to the eternal reward it is thus: inasmuch as works naturally follow faith, as I said, it is not necessary to command them, for it is impossible for faith not to do them without being commanded, in order that we may learn to distinguish the false from the true faith. Hence, the eternal reward also follows true faith, naturally, without any seeking, so that it is impossible that it should not, although it may never be desired or sought, yet it is appropriated and promised in order that true and false believers may be known, and that every one may understand that a good life follows naturally of itself.

As an illustration of this, take a rude comparison: behold, hell and death are also threatened to the sinner, and naturally follow sin without any seeking; for no one does wickedly because he wants to be damned, but would much rather escape it. Yet, the result is there, and it is not necessary to declare it, for it will come of itself. It is declared that man might know what follows a wicked life; so here, a wicked life has its own reward without seeking it. Hence, a good life will find its reward without any seeking it.

Now when Christ says, "make to yourselves friends," "lay up for yourselves treasures," and the like, you see that He means: do good, and it will follow of itself without your seeking, that you will have friends, find treasures in heaven, and receive a reward. But your eyes must simply be directed to a good life, and care nothing about the reward, but be satisfied to know and be assured that it will follow, and let God see to that. For those who look for a reward become lazy and unwilling laborers, and love the reward more than the work, yea, they become enemies of work. In this way God's will also becomes hateful, who has commanded us to work, and hence God's command and will must finally become burdensome to such a heart.

It Is Not the Saints, But God Only Who Receives Us Into the Everlasting Habitations, and Bestows the Reward

This is so clear that it needs no proof. For how can the saints receive us into heaven, as every one himself must depend on God alone to receive him into heaven, and every saint scarcely has enough for himself? This the wise virgins prove, who did not wish to give of their oil to the foolish virgins, and Peter says: "The righteous is scarcely saved." And Christ declares: "No man hath ascended up to heaven, but He that descended out of heaven, even the Son of Man, who is in heaven" (John 3:13).

What then shall we reply to: "Make to yourselves friends out of the mammon of unrighteousness; that, when it shall fail, they may receive you into the everlasting habitations?" We say this: That this passage says nothing about the saints in heaven, but of the poor and needy on earth, who live among us. As though Christ would say: "Why do you build churches, make saints and serve my mother, Peter, Paul and other departed saints? They do not need this or any other service of yours, they are not your friends, but friends of those who lived in their days and to whom they did good; but do service to your friends, that is, the poor who live in your time and among you, your nearest neighbors who need your help, make them your friends with your mammon."

Again, we must not understand this reception into the everlasting habitations as being done by man; however, man will be an instrument and witness to our faith, exercised and shown in their behalf, on account of which God receives us into the everlasting habitations. For thus the Scriptures are accustomed to speak when they say, sin condemns, faith saves; that means, sin is the cause why God condemns, and faith is the cause why He saves. As man also is at all times accustomed to say, your wickedness will bring you misfortune, which means, your wickedness is the cause and source of your misfortune. Thus our friends receive us into heaven, when they are the cause, through our faith shown to them, of entering heaven. This is enough on these three points.

What Is Mammon?

In this connection we will explain three questions, that we may better understand this Gospel. What is mammon? Why is it unrighteous? And why does Christ command us to imitate the unjust steward, who worked for his own gain at his master's expense, which without doubt is unjust and a sin?

First, *mammon is a Hebrew word meaning riches or temporal goods,* namely, whatever any one owns over and above what his needs require, and with which he can benefit others without injuring himself. For *hamon* in Hebrew means multitude, or a great crowd or many, from which mahamon or mammon, that is, multitude of riches or goods, is derived.

Second, *it is called unrighteous,* not because obtained by injustice and usury, for with unrighteous possessions no good can be done, for it must be returned, as Isaiah 61:8 says: "I, the Lord, love justice, I hate robbery with iniquity." And Solomon says: "Withhold not good from them to whom it is due, when it is in the power of thy hand to do it" (Proverbs 3:27). But it is called unrighteous because it stands in the service of unrighteousness, as Paul says to the Ephesians, that the days are evil, although God made them and they are good, but they are evil because wicked men misuse them, in which they do many sins, offend and endanger souls.

Therefore, riches are unrighteous, because the people misuse and abuse them. For we know that wherever riches are, the saying holds good: money rules the world, men creep for it, they lie for it, they act the hypocrite for it, and do all manner of wickedness against their neighbor to obtain it, to keep it, and increase it to possess the friendship of the rich.

But it is especially before God an unrighteous mammon because man does not serve his neighbor with it; for where my neighbor is in need and I do not help him when I have the means to do so, I unjustly keep what is his, as I am indebted to give to him according to the law of nature: "Whatever you would that men should do to you, do you even so to them" (Matthew 7:12). And again Christ says: "Give to him that asketh thee." And John in his first Epistle (1:17) says: "But whoso hath this world's goods, and seeth his brother have need, and shutteth up his bowels of compassion from him, how dwelleth the love of God in him?" And few see this unrighteousness in mammon because it is spiritual, and is found also in those possessions which are obtained by the fairest means, which deceive them that they think they do no one any harm, because they do no coarse outward injustice, by robbing, stealing and usury.

In the third place *it has been a matter of very great concern to many to know who the unjust steward is whom Christ so highly recommends?* This, in short, is the simple answer: Christ does not commend unto us the steward on account of his unrighteousness, but on account of his wisdom and his shrewdness, that with all his unrighteousness, he so wisely helps himself. As though I would urge some one to watch, pray and study, and would say: "Look here, murderers and thieves wake at night to rob and steal, why then do you not wake to pray and study?" By this I do not praise murderers and thieves for their crimes, but for the wisdom and foresight, that they so wisely obtain the goods of unrighteousness. Again, as though I would say: An unchaste woman adorns herself with gold and silk to tempt young men, why will you not also adorn yourself with faith to please Christ? By this I do not praise fornication, but the diligence employed.

In this way Paul compares Adam and Christ, saying: "Adam was a figure of him that was to come." Although from Adam we have nothing but sin, and from Christ nothing but grace, yet these are greatly opposed to each other. But the comparison and type consisted only in the consequences of birth, not in virtue or vice. As to birth, Adam is the father of all sinners, so Christ is the father of all the righteous. And as all sinners come from one Adam, so all the righteous come from one Christ. Thus the unjust steward is here typified to us *only* in his cunning and wisdom, who knows so well how to help himself, that we should also consider, in the right way, the welfare of our souls as he did, in the wrong way, that of his body and life. With this we will let it suffice, and pray God for grace.

NOTES

Faith's Approach to Christ

John Ker (1819-1886) is little known today, but in his day he was a respected preacher and professor of preaching and pastoral work at the United Free Church Seminary in Glasgow, Scotland. He published two volumes of sermons: this one is from the *Sermons First Series,* published in Edinburgh in 1870 by Edmonston and Douglas.

John Ker

7

FAITH'S APPROACH TO CHRIST

For she said within herself, If I may but touch his garment, I shall be whole (Matthew 9:21).

ONE ALWAYS LOVES to think of the surrounding circumstances of this miracle. Christ called to the ruler's house filled with mourning and death, with His heart absorbed in the great work which lay before Him, the first of the glancing proofs which He is to give that He is the resurrection and the life. The thronging press of the people is around Him, curious and expectant. But nothing far off or near, future or present, can shut out from Him the appeal of misery. He is, always and everywhere, alive to a suppliant's touch. His very garment, to its hem, is instinct with His own spirit and sensitive to the most trembling hand.

It is no less so now far up in heaven. The place which increases the sympathy of all hearts that enter there, has not diminished His. His garment, wide-spread and dropping low, is near our hand, and He feels a sinner's and a sufferer's touch upon His throne, with circle on circle of glory gathering round Him, and saints and angels thronging in. He came down that, in His nearness to our misery, we might learn to know His heart, and He arose that we might be assured of His power to help and heal. So let us seek to read this incident and consider what it teaches.

Faith Comes With a Deep Despair of All Other Help But Christ's

This woman had tried many means for many years. All that she possessed she had given, all that man will do for health she had done. She is not the better, but rather the worse. Hope had departed, which the poor sufferer surrenders last of all, and she is left to drag about a weary burden, and to feel that death only can unbind it.

But all this weakening of nature's hopes is that faith may rise to a hope above nature, to its Lord and God.

Had these past years of disappointment not brought her to the verge of despair, the great Physician would have been unsought.

Thus God will let the sinner or the sufferer wander on and try all other ways of cure, not to tantalize him with shadows, but to lead him through them to the great reality. He lets the prodigal go far away and deep down among the swine and the husks, and make experience of all man's friendships, such as they are in his poor circle, and find them all hollow and heartless, that his Father's house and face may rise glowing before him in the depth of his darkness, and he be driven to know them as never before. So He has permitted you perhaps to wander and exhaust all your strength and hope, sometimes on the world's pleasures, sometimes its moralities, sometimes on its business, sometimes its philosophy, and still to find the burden and the sore and the void, till, wearied in the greatness of your way, toil-worn and travel-sick, you say "There is no hope," that out of your despair this hope may rise like the morning-star out of black night. All other physicians have been tried, and you lie in your blood, that this question may be stirred—"Is there no balm in Gilead; is there no physician there?" (Jeremiah 8:22). Bless God for all failures if this vision at last rises, for despair itself, if such a hope is its child, for be sure that in God's world there are never shadows, except there is a reality from which they fall, and never failures in the soul's highest longings, but that they are steps to God, if the soul struggles on. Let your sin and sickness and sore lead to this name, "I am the Lord that healeth thee."

Faith Has a Divine Power to Discover Christ

We cannot tell what brought the woman to Him. It was in the beginning of His work, and we hear of no cure like hers before, none of any disease so deep and long-seated. Her ignorance and weakness, too, were great, and profound reasoning was not in her sphere of things. There was something in His look, His words, His whole personality, that drew her to Him, she could not tell why. But she came to Him.

"If I may but touch, I shall be whole,"—"I feel it, I know it."

And faith often goes so to Christ, straight to the mark like a driven arrow, with grounds for going that it cannot tell well to others, or tell even to itself. There is an intuition that has reasons in its heart, and that will be able to bring them out full and clear one day—a groping half-blind, which will yet find enlightened eyes,—a sense of misery, of sin, urged to Him by a divine necessity: "Lord, to whom shall we go? thou hast the words of eternal life" (John 6:68).

Can you tell why the compass needle trembles to the pole? the buds feel their way to the spring? the flowers to sunlight? They are made for it, and souls are so made for Christ. He created them, loved them, died for them, and when He comes near, they feel His presence and cannot live without Him. Would you know, deeper down, the ground of this? It is His whisper in the heart which has reached them: "My sheep hear my voice." "Jesus saith unto her, 'Mary.' She turned herself and saith unto Him, 'Rabboni,' which is to say, Master." Our appeal is only a response. The cure began with this woman before she touched. His arm guided hers. His strength sustained her weakness. His lips whisper to the soul, "Let us arise and go unto our Father;" and when we awake from our earthly sleep and see all things clear, we shall perceive that He was with us in all our best purposes, in our choosing and chosen hours; "God was in this place, and I knew it not." "Did not our heart burn within us, while He talked with us by the way?" It gives the assurance of final success in all who long for the healing of the soul, for where that soul feels its need and seeks a Christ, it is Christ who is there, leading it to Himself.

Faith Comes With an Implicit Trust in Christ

There were many things wanting and wrong in this woman's knowledge, but her faith was very full and absolute. Up to the measure of what she needed, her confidence was entire. Her faith is implicit in a *perfect cure:* "I shall be [not better, but] whole." It is implicit in His *ability:* "If I may but touch His garment." "The least contact with Him gives me all I need." How great the physician who could pour so complete a remedy through communication so slight!

May such implicit faith be ours! That up to the felt measure of our necessity, we should trust Christ with it all, and, when we discover more, trust Him with the increase,—that, with the growing sense of our sickness, we should believe there is power in Him to heal guilt and sorrow, and disappointment and doubt, and death itself,—that we shall yet be made *whole.* This requires faith, and seems to require it more, the longer that we live. Yet He will bestow this also. The faith is the promised gift of Him from whom it looks for the cure. "Lord, I believe, help thou mine unbelief."

And that our faith should be implicit in the ease with which He can accomplish it! A touch, a word, a thought from Him can do it. "Lord, if thou wilt, thou canst make me clean." "Speak the word only, and thy servant shall be made whole." For cures come from Christ as water from a fountain, light from the sun, life from the great God. They are the natural emanations that radiate from Him, hindered only by the obstructions which we interpose. If we could but realize this, in its full certainty, that the God who made us wills not our death, and that the Son of God is in our world to be the assurance and channel of this blessed will, delighting to do it, with what confidence might we draw near and receive out of His fulness grace for grace! If all hope for the soul were dead elsewhere, only that it might live in Him, as all our salvation—"Other refuge have I none, hangs my helpless soul on thee"—then would come the experience of those words, "My God shall supply all your need according to His riches in glory by Christ Jesus" (Philippians 4:19).

Faith Seeks, for its Comfort, Close Contact With Christ

"If I may but *touch.*" There is a trait of nature in this which gives us a sense of kinship. The heart seeks to press close to the Healer, as a sick child to its mother's breast. It is the instinct of suffering which Christ Himself has sanctioned. He took by the hand her who was sick of the fever; He touched the blind man's eyes, and put His fingers in the deaf man's ears. The sufferer and the Savior must be felt to be in contact, as necessary to our power to lay hold, if not to His ability to help.

It is in accordance with this that God weaves His attributes, the tokens of His presence, into all the works of His hands. He spreads His vesture abroad in creation, and brings it close to our touch, instinct with His being, that we may feel and grasp the God in whom we live and move, and know Him to be not a mere abstraction, but a God near and ever present. The incorporation of God in external nature is a step to His incarnation in human nature. It leads to that mysteriously intimate approach to us, when as "the children are partakers of flesh and blood," the eternal Son also "took part of the same." He put on the garment of humanity, and drew near in person, that we might clasp Him as a kinsman in our arms, and feel the infinite One to be our own. Our fallen nature made it needful that He should come closer still. He became the partaker of suffering and shame that we might touch Him in the sympathy of our hearts, and feel that, in like manner, He can touch us and be afflicted in all our afflictions. Nay more, He became sin for us, and bore it in our stead, that His healing touch might reach our conscience, and that we may have the assurance that He can be present to help in the deepest guilt and darkness of the soul.

The history of all God's dealings with man is the record of an approach nearer still, and nearer, until, in the incarnate Son, He shares all our sorrows, and carries our sins,—till faith puts its fingers into the print of the nails, its hand into the wounded side, and constrains us to cry, "My Lord, and my God."

So does He approach man, for man's heart thus yearns to draw near to Him—to a living God, to a personal Savior. We need this. We can believe a truth, but we can trust only a person,—we can admire a truth, we can love only a person,—we can meditate on a truth, we can commune only with a person, and faith stretches out a wistful hand to touch His garment that it may come at last to embrace Himself.

Faith, With All its Imperfections, Is Accepted by Christ

How imperfect this woman's faith was you can see. She thought she could be cured, and He not know. She imagined He healed by a sort of nature, not by a conscious act of will. In many, faith may be weak and ignorant, but touching Christ it is forgiven much. Like Samson, it is so full of faults and failure in itself, but when it turns to God, a divine power comes to it in its hour of need; and is not this the lesson of that strange Old Testament history?

What an encouragement to come to Christ truly, though it may be feebly, though conscious of many defects in our knowledge, creeping where we cannot walk, touching where we cannot lay hold! "He will not break the bruised reed, nor quench the smoking flax." And this gives us the hope that if a man really trusts God for one thing, he will be led on to more, from body to soul, from time to eternity. If we read rightly the 11th chapter of the Epistle to the Hebrews, we shall see that the writer teaches this. Those believers of the ancient Church cast themselves on God in some one crisis of their life, and this established the connection for ever. And if a man really and truly accepts of Christ in one part of His saving character, he will be led on, by the grace of God, to accept Him in all. For Christ is one, and instinct in every part of His nature with the life that heals. Let us thank God if we feel in ourselves, or see in any man, a thorough faith in some one side of the helping and healing power of the Son of God. It is no reason why we should rest in what is partial, but abundant reason why we should be encouraged to maintain our hold. If we grasp the garment-hem we shall bring Him to turn the face, and to say, "Be of good comfort, thy faith hath made thee whole" (Matthew 9:22).

Faith Feels a Change From the Touch of Christ

"And she felt in her body that she was healed" (Mark 5:29). There was an inward sense, which could not be mistaken, of return to wholeness—the stanching of a wound through which life, for long years, had been slowly ebbing, and the rising of a tide of new existence which made her feel she could yet be, and do, something in God's world. It is almost worth years of weary wasting to have one hour of the blessed consciousness. The dew of youth comes back, the world seems to put on sunshine and springtime in sympathy, as if God were making it all anew, and the man, who was lying like a crushed and helpless worm, rejoices in the thought of the hard duties and heavy burdens which come to try his fresh-created strength.

When faith, under a sense of its need, touches Christ, the virtue that comes from Him gives some such feeling to the soul. When that great transference of sin and spiritual sickness is made to the Savior the soul is safe, entirely and eternally safe, through the grace of Him who will keep that soul which we commit to His trust, and who will never suffer any one to pluck it out of His hand. There is a crisis of this kind in every spiritual history, if the new life is to begin—some turning-point in the disease where it sets in to hope and health! We do not say that, in the spiritual frame, there is always the same full and immediate sense of it. In most cases not, for the soul's recovery is very gradual and fitful, even though it is sure, and, in some cases, the struggle of doubt is part of the process through which it gains at last its highest power. But this will prevail in the midst of all, a feeling of change, of something new and hopeful, when Christ is looked to and leaned upon, a sense of contact with a power out of, and above, the world, which can give life and courage for the soul's sorest battles, and which whispers to it, often with sure conviction that it shall prevail.

There are men in whose presence you feel strength and comfort, whose look and words are like a reinforcement to turn the battle from the gate. Have you this feeling, above all, when your heart rises to the thought of that august and godlike Presence, when it seeks that "blessed and gracious face?" Then take courage. The pressing throng of doubts and fears, of worldly cares and temptations, may thrust aside, at times, the hand that touches, but do not turn away. "In returning and rest shall ye be saved!" The thrill of life which comes from Him tells of far more yet to be gained. "He is come that we might have life, and that we might have it more abundantly" (John 10:10). He will bring into contact not only with His garment but with His heart, and then the peace that fills it, and the joy that overflows it, shall be the portion of those who lay hold of Him. They shall know "the love of Christ which passeth knowledge, that they may be filled with all the fulness of God" (Ephesians 3:19)!

For this end Christ has entered the world, that He may make man the heir of God and God the heritage of man. He stands before us more clearly now, that He may assure us of it. He has borne the penalty of sin, has passed through death in our nature, and has risen above it, bearing those marks of His suffering which prove His continued share in our humanity and His everlasting sympathy with us. "Behold my hands and my feet, that it is I myself: handle me and see" (Luke 24:39). And He shows us His hands and His feet.

At a communion table it would seem as if the Savior were bringing His garment-hem nearer to our hand, that touch may aid faith, and His person stands before us through visible memorials. Our eyes are made to see, our hands to handle, and our lips to taste, the Word of life, that He, whose we are, may enter our soul by every gateway, and take our nature into full possession.

Christ is now, as He was then, passing through the midst of men, if they would but see Him. Still, they throng and press and draw nothing from Him, because they bring no eye to discern, and do not feel that need which opens the eyesight. We can take from Him only what we perceive in Him, and must urge the prayer that "God would reveal His Son in us!"

For this, too, He has provided. Though the Head be far away, by His Spirit He comes near. "He shall take of mine and show it unto you." It is the holy oil, poured on the head, which descends even to the skirts of His garments, to His border's utmost hem, to every symbol and to every suppliant, to put healing power into the fainting heart, and to "fill the house with the odor of the ointment."

It is our hope and joy to think, as we touch Him here, with the hands of dying men, that He is still, as once before, passing on through the world to perform His greatest work: to raise the dead. Many a home like that of Jairus looks for His appearing. Himself the Risen One, He is advancing to awaken His friends who have fallen asleep, and to comfort those who mourn over them, and who wait for His coming. He spreads His garment, meanwhile, as He moves, to the touch of misery and sin, and if He lingers in His progress to the homes of the dead, it is but to gather in His train the fuller fruits of His redeeming toil. His mercy and our need cause the seeming delay. His work on the way must be finished ere the close can come, that close so longed for by all fainting spirits and bereaved hearts. Sinner, sufferer, while you are in the way with Him, touch Him and follow. Ere long He will enter that highest house, and you possess the privilege of the best-beloved, to enter the innermost chamber with Him, where sorrow shall be turned into joy and death into life, where faith which touches the hem shall rise to vision that beholds the face, and friends who part and weep at nightfall shall meet at day-dawn, in a world where the voice of crying shall not be heard any more, nor the shadow of death fall upon the heart forever.

A Growing Faith

Amzi Clarence Dixon (1854-1925) was a Baptist preacher who ministered to several congregations in the South before becoming pastor of the Moody Memorial Church in Chicago (1906-11). He left Chicago to pastor the famous Metropolitan Tabernacle in London, "Spurgeon's Tabernacle" (1911-19). He died in 1925 while pastoring the University Baptist Church, Baltimore, Maryland. A close associate of Reuben A. Torrey, Dixon helped him edit *The Fundamentals.* Dixon was a popular preacher in both Britain and America.

A. C. Dixon

8

A GROWING FAITH

. . . And the man believed the word that Jesus had spoken unto him. . . (John 4:50).

FEW THINGS ARE more interesting than the growth of a child, body and mind, from infancy to manhood; but more interesting still is the growth of the new child, the result of the second birth—growth from spiritual infancy to spiritual manhood. And in the text and context we have a growth like this. Weak faith has become strong faith. We shall trace this growth, and learn, if we can, the secret by which weak faith may become strong. Let us examine (1) The signs of a weak faith and (2) The signs of a strong faith.

The Signs of a Weak Faith

They are four:

1. *Demanding visible proof.* "Except ye see signs and wonders," said Jesus, "ye will not believe" (John 4:48). We desire to see. "Seeing is believing," says the old proverb; and yet we may be deceived through sight more readily than through almost any other sense. Faith based upon sight is very weak. "The devils believe and tremble" (James 2:19). They see evidences of God's power which they cannot deny, and they tremble before it. It is really unbelief which demands visible proof. It was the unbelief of Thomas which made him say, "I will not believe till I see." And Jesus rebuked him when He said, "Blessed are they that have not seen and yet have believed" (John 20:25, 29). Said the rich man in Hades: "Send Lazarus that he may tell my five brethren not to come to this place of torment; if one rise from the dead they will believe." "No," said Abraham; "if they hear not Moses and the prophets, neither will they be persuaded though one rose from the dead" (Luke 16:27-31). And if I, through the power of God, could raise from the dead every corpse in Greenwood Cemetery, and march the living men and women through the streets, Brooklyn

would not believe. Men who will not hear God as He speaks through the Bible will not hear Him when He speaks through miracles.

2. *Another sign of weak faith is that it must be driven to God by overwhelming need.* This nobleman's son was at the point of death. Every physician had doubtless been tried, and the most skillful had given up the case. In this time of great distress the father thinks of Jesus, and starts for Him. It is like a man on a vessel in a storm at sea, when he feels the timbers cracking beneath him, and imagines the depth to which he may soon sink, calling out, "Lord, have mercy upon me!" It is like the soldier's cry, so often heard in battle, when he feels the bullet strike him: "Lord, have mercy!" It is like repentance on a deathbed—the sailor throwing all the goods overboard in a tempest, and then seeking to gather them up in the calm that follows.

Such faith is better than no faith, but it is not so good as the faith that draws us to God by gratitude and love. It is better to be driven than not to come at all; it is still better to be drawn. Doubtless this nobleman had heard of Christ many times; but he did not go to Him. He may have had opportunities to invite Him to his house, but he did not improve them. Not until the great sorrow comes, which he hopes Jesus may relieve, does he come to Him at all. Zaccheus, on the other hand, invited the Lord to dine with him, when there was no sorrow to be relieved. His faith was, therefore, better than that of the nobleman.

Matthew invited the Lord to a feast at his house. He wished Him to share his joys. And such faith strikes me as of a higher order than that which drives us by sheer force of distress to seek relief from Christ.

3. *A third sign of weak faith is that, while it prays, it dictates to God.* This father besought Jesus that He would *come down* and heal his son. He does not make known his wants and leave to Christ the manner in which they shall be supplied. He wants Christ to come to his house. I think I perceive the tone of patronage in this invitation. A nobleman rarely ever forgets that he is a nobleman, and he says to himself, "Only the rabble have

honored Jesus. I will now invite Him to my mansion, and be the first among the nobility to show Him respect, if He will come and heal my son"—a spirit just the opposite of the centurion's, who said, "I am not worthy that Thou shouldst come beneath my roof: but speak the word, and my servant shall be healed" (Matthew 8:8).

Here humility dictates to Christ; but He accepts the dictation neither of patronizing pride nor of great humility. He goes uninvited to the centurion's house, and heals his servant. He refuses to go, though invited, to the nobleman's house, while He heals his son with a word. Perfect faith does not dictate to God, but much of our praying consists in this humble or patronizing dictation. We try to convince God that He is wrong in His way of doing, and we are right. Though we are greatly shocked by the blasphemy recently uttered: "If I had been present at the creation, I could have given God some advice; or, if He would consult me as to how to govern the world, I could help Him in it,"—yet we sometimes show a spirit distressingly similar.

Some tenants were ejected from a large building in New York City some time ago. They tried to get back in, for it was cold out on the streets; but the police refused to let them enter. The reason of their refusal was that the building was about to tumble down, and they knew that for the good of the tenants it was better that they should suffer the cold than be exposed to the danger from the falling walls. And yet these tenants persisted in trying to escape the cold by putting themselves in danger. They thought they knew better than the police. The result showed that the police were the wiser. And the result will always show that God's dealings with us, though they may seem to be severe, are wise and good.

John Wesley had two preachers under his direction, named Bradburn and Duncan. Bradburn was a very eloquent man; Duncan was a rather poor preacher. When Bradburn preached, Duncan tried to be present; but when Duncan preached, Bradburn was usually absent, and it distressed Duncan. Finally he asked his Brother Bradburn why it was he did not come to hear him preach. "To tell the truth," replied Bradburn, "I cannot hear you without being greatly tempted." "And what, pray," said Duncan, "is the nature of the temptation?" "I am always tempted to think," said Bradburn, "that I can preach better than you, and it ministers to my pride." Such is the feeling of Brother Weakfaith toward God. He has the impression that he could do better than the Lord, if he had the whole thing in hand; and it is a temptation which he needs to resist.

4. *The fourth sign of a weak faith is its impatience.* This father evidently became impatient: "Sir, come down ere my child die."

There is something almost of petulance in this request. It shows that he thinks it is no time now to argue. What he wants is haste, and he cannot brook delay. Our impatience with God is a sign of very weak faith.

It is comforting to know that Jesus honors even faith like this. Though impatient and dictatorial, driven by need and seeking visible evidence, He answers the prayer. He pities our weakness. "The bruised reed He will not break; the smoking flax He will not quench." The fire of trust does not blaze up; He sees more of the smoke of impatience and unbelief than of faith, but He will not allow the sparks beneath the flax to be trampled out. The reed of our faith is very weak, but He will not allow the bird that would break it to light upon it. Indeed, He fans the sparks into a flame; He puts new life into the reed that will heal the bruises and make it strong.

A New Jersey farmer one morning heard a little wren pouring out its heart in song upon the early air. Now and then it would stop as if interrupted, and by and by continue its song again. Drawing near he noticed that the mother was teaching her young to sing. She would first sing through the whole song, and then listen to the little one sing, until it broke down, and then she would take up the song and carry it through. This was repeated until the little birds could sing the mother's song accurately. And when we break down in our song of faith, God delights to take up the strain and help us through. His strength is made perfect in our weakness; all that we lack He supplies.

You may have heard John B. Gough tell, in one of his thrilling lectures, of a scene in his own experience. Sitting in a church one morning, he heard a hoarse, discordant voice behind him, and he felt sorry that he was near such a disagreeable creature. The preacher announced the hymn, "Just as I am, without one plea," and the discordant voice, without any melody or much tune, followed the words. While the interlude was being played before the second verse, Mr. Gough felt a hand touch his arm, and a voice saying: "Please, sir, what is the next verse? Tell me the first line: I think I might remember it." "Just as I am, poor, wretched, blind," said Gough, and, as he looked into the stranger's face saw that he was blind. And when he heard him with his grating voice trying to sing the next lines,

> Sight, riches, healing of the mind,
> Yea, all I need in Thee to find,
> O Lamb of God! I come.

Gough said he felt that he would like to lend him what voice he had, and help him to sing if he could. And so God feels toward us when we try to serve or to believe. He would help us in our failures, and, unlike Gough, He is able to do it. He can give us just what we need. Christ honored the weak faith of this father in order that his weak faith might become strong.

This leads us to:

The Signs of a Strong Faith

They, too, are four:

1. *Faith in the Word of God.* The text tells us that "the man believed the word that Jesus had spoken" (John 4:50). He no longer desired a sign; he could now rely upon the simple word. There was something in the tone of the voice, in the magnetic presence, as well as in what Jesus said, which went to his heart and gave him faith. And so there is something in this Word of God—a living something which goes with it and helps us to believe. I have no superstitious feeling toward the Bible. I do not regard its binding, its paper, its ink, its material make-up, as especially sacred. *Webster's Dictionary* is

as good a book to dream by and tell fortunes by as the Bible. It is no fetish. The truth in it is the sacred thing. What it means is hallowed ground. We may treat the Bible as the patient treated the prescription of the doctor, who told him to put it in a little water, and take it according to directions; and when the doctor returned the next day, he found the patient worse. "Have you taken my prescription?" he asked. "Yes, just as you told me. Here it is," and he handed him a glass of water in which the paper had been dissolved; and he had taken several spoonfuls of paper-pulp for medicine. Instead of doing what the prescription told him, he simply took the prescription itself. In that sense "the letter killeth."

The truth of God, ever living, is sacred. I like the spirit of the man who refused to let any book in his house lie upon the Bible. He regarded it as above all books, and hence none of his children could lay their books upon it. A wise reverence for the Book is not out of place. But what I insist upon is that what the Book means is more than the book itself.

The words of God are very precious, and we learn to revel in the truth itself apart from any benefit that we receive from it. A house-decorator in Buffalo, New York, was ordered to paper every room but one, and he was curious to know why that room was left blank. On entering, however, he saw a strange scene. On the walls were pasted hundreds of letters, and the young lady, who was kept within doors much of her time, said that she had thus papered the walls of her room because every letter was precious to her heart. There were letters from mother, now in heaven; from friends in the skies; letters which brought up pleasant associations of childhood and school-days. Every one of them had a meaning to her; she could sit in her room and revel in these associations. And so we may have our rooms of memory filled with Scripture truths. Every one of them is suggestive of something in the past, the remembrance of which gives us delight. This one tells of victory won; that one of a sorrow borne; another of a perplexity in which we were guided; another still of some great calamity which might have crushed us but for the promise that sustained. No man can prize the Word of God too highly and depend upon it too implicitly.

2. *Another sign of strong faith is restfulness.* This father came from home in great haste, and he was impatient at the delay of Jesus, but after Jesus had said "Thy son liveth," we find him in no hurry. Not until next day does he start for home. He believes that his son is cured, and there is no need of hurry. Having watched, perhaps, at the bedside of his sick boy for many nights, he decides to stay in Capernaum and have a good night's rest. He sleeps until late in the morning, when he quietly takes his breakfast, and then starts leisurely toward home. The wife is uneasy about him: "Why does husband stay away so long? He, of course, does not know that our child is well;" and calling the servant she says, "Go up to Cana, and tell husband the joyful news;" and as they come he meets them, and hears from them without surprise the account of the healing. It is hardly news to him.

"He that believeth maketh not haste" (Isaiah 28:16). He rests upon God with a quiet heart. He is willing to let God take His time, confident that God's time is better than his. He has the promise, which to the eye of faith is equal to the fulfillment. He has already entered upon the enjoyment of what is promised. The Holy of Holies is his, described by the words: "Thou wilt keep him in perfect peace whose mind is stayed on Thee, because he trusteth in Thee" (Isaiah 26:3). In this age of hurry, we need such a rest of faith.

3. *A third sign of strong faith is its readiness to receive confirmation.* As the father goes homeward, he hears the echo of the words which Jesus spoke. The servants use the very language of Jesus. Jesus had said: "Thy son liveth." The servants say: "Thy son liveth." You have stood, perhaps, in the pisa Baptistry in Italy, or on Echo Lake in New York, and heard your words brought back just as you spoke them. But an echo like this which the nobleman heard is sweeter than all the echoes in nature. The man who believes God's Word will hear, sooner or later, the echo of answer. He will hear it in fulfillment of some kind. "Faithful is He who has

promised" (Hebrews 10:23). And you will notice how ready the nobleman was to receive the confirmation of his faith. He compared the time when Christ spoke the word with the time when his son was healed, and he saw it was the same hour. Now unbelief would have suggested: "This is a remarkable coincidence, to be sure; but there is no necessary connection between the words of Jesus and the healing. He might have gotten well anyhow." And so, when we have asked and received, the temptation too often is to take honor from God by giving credit to secondary causes. The tempter suggests: "You have what you wanted, but it might have come even without praying for it." Such is the attitude of unbelief. Faith stands ready to be confirmed by the testimony of others, and by a direct answer to a definite petition.

4. *The last sign of strong faith we will mention is its willingness to receive spiritual blessing.* We are told that the nobleman "himself believed, and all his house." The first thing he did, doubtless, when he reached home, was to search out the old Scriptures and read of the Messiah. And turning to his boy with eyes now bright with intelligence and cheeks flushed with health, he says, "You have been saved from death by the Great Physician. Are you willing now to trust Him as your Savior from sin?" And looking into the face of his wife, he says, "Will you also trust Him?" And then turning to the other children and the servants, he gets a promise from all that they will trust the Savior. And kneeling now with the open scroll of the Scriptures before him, he returns thanks to God for the blessing of the child restored—better still, of a household redeemed. He has received from Jesus more than he asked. He came for the healing of his son; he has received the healing of his whole family. He came for temporal blessing; he has received spiritual blessing. He came anxious that the home on earth might be happy; he has received a home in heaven made happier. Such is God's way of dealing. He knows how to give above all we can ask or think. Great faith prizes spiritual above temporal blessings, and has the

secret by which the temporal is transmuted into the eternal.

I now appeal to every one who has been blessed of God in body, in family, in any respect. Will you not, like this nobleman and his family, permit these temporal blessings to bring to you spiritual blessings? Will you not in gratitude give your hearts to Christ? The king asked John Fletcher of Madeley, "What do you desire that I may give you?" "I want," replied Fletcher, "only more grace." The faith that seeks the spiritual is above the faith that seeks only the temporal.

The Shield of Faith

John Henry Jowett (1864-1923) was known as "the greatest preacher in the English-speaking world." Born in Yorkshire, England, he was ordained into the Congregational ministry. His second pastorate was at the famous Carr's Lane Church, Birmingham, where he followed the eminent Dr. Robert W. Dale. From 1911-18, he pastored the Fifth Avenue Presbyterian Church, New York City; and from 1918-23, he ministered at Westminster Chapel, London, succeeding G. Campbell Morgan. He wrote many books of devotional messages and sermons. This message comes from *The Whole Armour of God,* published in 1916 by Fleming H. Revell.

John Henry Jowett

9

THE SHIELD OF FAITH

> Above all, taking the shield of faith, wherewith ye shall be able to quench all the fiery darts of the wicked (Ephesians 6:16).

BUT DID THE APOSTLE Paul who gives this counsel find his faith an all-sufficient shield? He recommends the shield of faith, but is the recommendation based on personal experience? And if so, what is the nature and value of that experience? What sort of protection did his faith give to him? When I examine his life, what tokens do I find of guardianship and strong defense? When I move through the ways of his experience, is it like passing through quiet and shady cloisters shut away from the noise and heat of the fierce and feverish world? Is his protected life like a garden walled around, full of sweet and pleasant things, and secured against the maraudings of robber and beast?

Let us look at this protected life. Let us glance at the outer circumstances. Here is one glimpse of his experience:

> Of the Jews five times received I forty stripes save one.... Once was I stoned, thrice have I suffered shipwreck, a day and a night have I been in the deep; . . . in stripes above measure, in prisons more frequent, in deaths oft, in weariness and painfulness, in watchings often, in hunger and thirst, in fastings often, in cold and nakedness (2 Corinthians 11:24-27).

And yet this is the man who speaks about the shield of faith, and in spite of the protecting shield all these things happened unto him!

Look at his bodily infirmities. "There was given unto me a thorn in the flesh" (2 Corinthians 12:7). Where was the shield? It is not necessary for us to know the character of his thorn. But assuredly it was some ailment which appeared to interfere with the completeness of his work. Some think it was an affliction of the eyes; others think that it was a proneness to some form of malarial fever which frequently brought him into a state of collapse and exhaustion. But there it was, and the shield of faith did not keep it away.

Or, *look again at his exhausting labors.* There is no word concerning his ministry more pregnant with meaning than this word "labor," which the apostle so frequently used to describe his work. "In labors oft;" "whereunto I labor;" "I labored more abundantly than they all." This is not the labor of ordinary toil. It is the labor of travail. It is labor to the degree of poignant pang. It is labor that so expends the strength as to empty the fountain. It is the labor of sacrifice. And I thought that perhaps a protected life might have been made fruitful without pain. I thought God might have protected His servant, but the shield of faith did not deliver him from the labor of travail through which he sought the birth of the children of grace.

Or, *look once more at his repeated failures.* You can hear the wail of sadness as he frequently contemplates his ruined hopes concerning little churches which he had built, or concerning fellow-believers whom he had won to Christ. "Are ye so soon fallen away?" "Ye would have given your eyes to me but now. . . ." "I hear that there is strife among you." "It is reported that there is uncleanness among you." "Demus hath forsaken me." And it is wail after wail, for it is failure after failure. Defeat is piled upon defeat. It is declared to be a protected life, and yet disasters litter the entire way. It is perfectly clear that the shield of faith did not guard him from the agony of defeat.

Such are the experiences of the man who gave his strength to proclaim the all-sufficiency of the shield of faith, who spent his days in recommending it to his fellow-men, and whose own life was, nevertheless, noisy with tumult, and burdened with antagonisms, and crippled by infirmity, and clouded with defeat. Can this life be said to be wearing a shield? We have so far been looking at the man's environment, at his bodily infirmities, at his activities of labor, at his external defeats. What if in all these things we have not come within sight of the realm which the apostle would describe as his life?

When Paul speaks of life he means the life of the soul.

When he thinks of life his eyes are on the soul. In all the estimates and values which he makes of life he is fixedly regarding the soul. The question of success or failure in life is judged by him in the courthouse of the soul. You cannot entice the apostle away to life's accidents and induce him to take his measurements there. He always measures life with the measurement of an angel, and thus he busies himself not with the amplitude of possessions, but with the quality of being, not with the outer estates of circumstances but with the central keep and citadel of the soul. We never find the apostle Paul with his eyes glued upon the wealth or poverty of his surroundings. But everywhere and always and with endless fascination, he watches the growth or decay of the soul. When, therefore, this man speaks of the shield of faith we may be quite sure that he is still dwelling near the soul and that he is speaking of a protection which will defend the innermost life from foul and destructive invasion.

Living Without the Shield of Faith

Now our emphasis is prone to be entirely the other way, and, therefore, we are very apt to misinterpret the teachings of the apostle Paul and to misunderstand the holy promises of the Lord. We are prone to live in the incidents of life rather than in its essentials, in environment rather than in character, in possessions rather than in dispositions, in the body rather than in the soul. The consequence is that we seek our shields in the realms in which we live. We live only in the things of the body and, therefore, against bodily ills we seek our shields. We want a shield against sorrow, to keep it away, a shield against the darkening eclipse of the sunny day. We want a shield against loss, to keep it away, a shield against the rupture of pleasant relations, a shield to protect us against the bereavements which destroy the completeness of our fellowships. We want a shield against pain, to keep it away, a shield against the pricks and goads of piercing circumstances, against the slings and arrows of outrageous fortune.

In a word, we want a shield to make us comfortable,

and because the shield of faith does not do it we are often stunned and confused, and our thin reasonings are often twisted and broken, and the world appears a labyrinth without a providence and without a plan. It is just here that our false emphasis leads us astray. We live in circumstances and seek a shield to make us comfortable; but the apostle Paul lived in character and sought a shield to make him holy. He was not concerned with the arrangement of circumstances, but he was concerned with the aspiration that, be the circumstances what they might, they should never bring disaster to his soul. He did not seek a shield to keep off ill-circumstances, but he sought a shield to keep ill-circumstances from doing him harm. He sought a shield to defend him from the destructiveness of every kind of circumstance, whether fair or foul, whether laden with sunshine or heavy with gloom. Paul wanted a shield against all circumstances in order that no circumstance might unman him and impoverish the wealth of his soul.

Let me offer a simple illustration. A ray of white light is made up of many colors, but we can devise screens to keep back any one of these colors and to let through those we please. We can filter the rays. Or we can devise a screen to let in rays of light and to keep out rays of heat. We can intercept certain rays and forbid their presence. Now, to the apostle Paul the shield of faith was a screen to intercept the deadly rays which dwell in every kind of circumstance; and to Paul the deadly rays in circumstances, whether the circumstances were bright or cloudy, were just those that consumed his spiritual susceptibilities and lessened his communion with God, the things that ate out his moral fiber, and that destroyed the wholeness and wholesomeness of his human sympathies, and impaired his intimacy with God and man. It was against these deadly rays he needed a shield, and he found it in the shield of faith.

Paul wanted a shield, not against failure; that might come or stay away. But he wanted a shield against the pessimism that may be born of failure, and which holds the soul in the fierce bondage of an Arctic winter. Paul wanted a shield, not against injury; that might come or stay away; but against the deadly thing that is born of injury, even the foul offspring of revenge. Paul wanted a shield, not against pain; that might come or might not come; he sought a shield against the spirit of murmuring which is so frequently born of pain, the deadly, deadening mood of complaint. Paul wanted a shield, not against disappointment, that might come or might not come; but against the bitterness that is born of disappointment, the mood of cynicism which sours the milk of human kindness and perverts all the gentle currents of the soul. Paul wanted a shield, not against difficulty; that might come or might not come; but against the fear that is born of difficulty, the cowardice and the disloyalty which are so often bred of stupendous tasks. Paul did not want a shield against success; that might come or might not come; but against the pride that is born of success, the deadly vanity and self-conceit which scorch the fair and gracious things of the soul as a prairie-fire snaps up a homestead or a farm. Paul did not want a shield against wealth; that might come or might not come; but against the materialism that is born of wealth, the deadly petrifying influence which turns flesh into stone, spirituality into benumbment, and which makes a soul unconscious of God and of eternity. The apostle did not want a shield against any particular circumstance, but against every kind of circumstance, that in everything he might be defended against the fiery darts of the devil.

The Faith-Life

He found the shield he needed in a vital faith in Christ. First of all, *the faith-life cultivates the personal fellowship of the Lord Jesus Christ.* The ultimate concern of faith is not with a polity, not with a creed, not with a church, and not with a sacrament, but with the person of the Lord Jesus Christ. Therefore, the first thing we have to do if we wish to wear the shield of faith is to cultivate the companionship of the Lord. We must seek His holy presence. We must let His purpose enter into and possess our minds. We must let His promises distil into our hearts. And we must let our own hearts and minds dwell upon the loved ones who have gone from our side. We must talk to Him in secret and we must let Him talk to us. We must consult Him about our affairs, and then take His counsels as our statutes, and pay such heed to them that the statutes will become our songs. Faith-life cultivates the friendship of Christ, and leans upon it, and surrenders itself with glorious abandon to the sovereign decrees of His grace and love.

And secondly, *the faith-life puts first things first, and in its list of primary values it gives first place to the treasures of the soul.* Faith-life is more concerned with habits than with things, with character than with office, with self-respect than with popular esteem. The faith-life puts first things first, the clean mind and the pure heart, and from these it never turns its eyes away.

And lastly, *the faith-life contemplates the campaign rather than the single battle.* One battle may seem to go against it. But faith knows that one battle is not the end of the world. "I will see you again, and your sorrow shall be turned into joy." Faith takes the long view, the view of the entire campaign. "I saw the holy city, the new Jerusalem, coming down out of heaven from God." "The kingdoms of this world shall become the kingdom of our God." Such a relationship to the Lord protects our life as with an invincible shield. It may please God to conduct our life through long reaches of cloudless noon; the shield of faith will be our defense. It may please God to lead us through the gloom of a long and terrible night; the shield of faith will be our defense. "Thou shalt not be afraid . . . of the pestilence that walketh in darkness, nor for the destruction that wasteth at noonday" (Psalm 91:6).

NOTES

The Leisure of Faith

George H. Morrison (1866-1928) assisted the great Alexander Whyte in Edinburgh, pastored two churches, and then became pastor in 1902 of the distinguished Wellington Church on University Avenue in Glasgow. His preaching drew great crowds; in fact, people had to queue up an hour before the services to be sure to get seats in the large auditorium. Morrison is a master of imagination in preaching, yet his messages are solidly biblical. From his many published volumes of sermons, I have chosen this message, found in *Sun-Rise: Addresses From a City Pulpit,* published in 1903 by Hodder and Stoughton, London.

George H. Morrison

10

THE LEISURE OF FAITH

... He that believeth shall not make haste (Isaiah 28:16).

I THINK WE shall all agree that in the life of our modern cities there is recognizable the note of haste. One has only to watch one of our crowded streets to detect the pressure at the back of life. Life is more urgent than it used to be, the tranquility of an older day is passing. The stream had still and shadowed reaches in it once, but today it hurries forward very swiftly.

Now it is notable that with that greater haste there is found, without any question, a lesser faith. There is a certain shrinking of the faculty of faith in the organism of our complex life. I am no pessimist, and I trust that none of you are. Life, for all its sorrow, is too real, too deep, too rich, to write that name of failure on its brow. But the most cheerful optimist cannot be blind to this, that faith, and reverence which is the child of faith, are not conspicuous on our modern cities; and the singular thing is, that with that decline of faith we should have witnessed the increase of hurry. Did you ever think that these features were connected? The Bible affirms it in the clearest manner. You say that the absence of restfulness in modern life springs from the fierce struggle for existence. But the Bible goes a great deal deeper than that: *the want of rest is rooted in want of trust.* Depend upon it, he that believeth *not* is always in danger of feverish impatience. Depend upon it, that to the end of time, he that believeth shall not make haste.

Of course, it is very necessary for clear thinking to distinguish the haste of our text from strenuous speed. Every one who is at all in earnest about things feels the push and the pull to get his life-work done; but a strenuous and resolute forwardness such as that is very different from the spirit of haste. "Unhasting but unresting" should be the motto on every Christian's coat of arms. It is impossible that a true Christian should be a sluggard. Such new conceptions of life have dawned on him. Duty, service, and the building up of character are so expanded when God has touched the soul, that as with the stirring music of the trumpet we are called to redeem the time because the days are evil. But the man who hastes never redeems the time. You never redeem anything by hurrying. And it is of that impatience, so closely akin to fickleness—and an age of hurry is extraordinarily fickle—it is of that impatience which knows no inward quietude, and which robs life of its music and its march, that the prophet is speaking here. He that believeth shall run and not be weary. He that believeth shall press toward the mark. He that believeth—God to his tardy feet has promised to lend the swiftness of the roe. But in spite of that—no, because of that—he that believeth shall not make haste.

Hasty Judgments

I like to apply our text to hasty judgments. He that believeth shall not make haste to judge. It is amazing how rashly and how recklessly we pass severe judgments on each other. There is nothing harder than suspense of judgment in our daily intercourse with men and women. Even the kindliest are in danger of prejudging, and those who are not kindly do so constantly. Now do you see how we are to escape that sin? Do you observe the secret of suspended judgment? It is not a matter of caution after all, for he that believeth shall not make haste to judge. In all disparagement there is a lack of faith. In every hasty summing up of character what is really revealed is our own want of trust. If we only believed in our brother a little more, if we only credited the divine within him; if we only realized that under the outward man there is a hidden man of the heart striving and struggling, we should be readier to think more kindly than we do. I want you to believe that under all disguise there is a spark of the divine fire in every heart. I want you to believe that God is not far away even from the life that you and I call godless. He that believeth in the love and patience of Heaven, and in the image of God, defaced but not destroyed, will not make haste to judge.

Enjoy Life's Pleasures

Again, I think our text is full of meaning for those who are in a great hurry to enjoy, and perhaps the haste to be rich and taste life's pleasures was never so markedly felt as it is now. It is always a difficult thing to wait. David was never more saintly in his life than just when he waited patiently for God. But today, when the means of enjoyment are so multiplied and the music of the world is doubly sweet, the monotony of duty has become doubly irksome. It is very hard to be bound to that desk all day, while the golden hours of youth are flying so quickly. It is very hard from morning till weary night to be standing behind the counter in the store, when life might be so rich and many-colored if only there were a little liberty and leisure.

Has not one of our own poets, himself a minister of the gospel, sung, "Gather the rosebuds while ye may, old time is still aflying?" Hence springs a certain rebellion at our lot, a craving for immediate satisfaction; a bitter willingness to forget the morrow if only we can snatch some pleasure now; and to all men and women who are tempted so—and multitudes are tempted so today—comes the stern word of the eternal God, "He that believeth shall not make haste." The modern catechism asks, "What is man's chief end?" and the answer it gives is "Man's chief end is to enjoy *life*." But the older catechism was wiser when it answered, "Man's chief end is to enjoy *God*," and God can only be enjoyed, be sure of it, in the sphere of duty and along the line of work. Outside of that, the presence of God is lost, and the cup is always bitter when that is lost. Life has not been given us to enjoy, life has been given us to *use;* and I fancy you can use it better where you are, than if you had your own sweet will tomorrow. However grey and cheerless duty is, a man must trample down his moods and do it. Then, in God's time, far sooner than we dream the richest joys will reach us unexpectedly, and life will unfold itself, out of the mists, into a thing of beauty and a joy forever. He that believeth can say, "Get thee behind me, Satan." He that believeth will not make haste.

Wait to See Results

Again, I keep whispering this text within my heart, when I observe our common haste to see results. The man who believes in himself and in his message is never in a hurry to see results. It is always a mark of inferior capacity to be in a feverish hurry to be recognized. No genius ever goes to sleep with the wild hope that tomorrow he may wake up famous. Genius is sublimely confident and easy; with the touch of God-given power comes sweet assurance. What I feel is that if the church of Christ really believes in her mission and her message, she must not be feverish about results. I think it is more often faithlessness than faith that clamors for immediate statistics. The purposes of Heaven are very long, and God fulfills Himself in many ways. The soul of man is infinitely delicate, and you can never tabulate the powers that touch it. Be not weary in well-doing. You see no fruit? So be it. Remember that with your Lord a thousand years are as a single day. He that believeth is strong to sow in tears, but he shall not make haste to reap in joy.

God Never Hurries

Now when we turn to the dealings of God with men there is one thing that impresses us very deeply. It is the slowness of all God's procedure in guiding and blessing our humanity. God never hurries; He moves with infinite ease. He takes an age to perfect one of His thoughts within us. What I might call the leisureliness of providence is written large on human history. Think of the weary discipline of Israel till they had grasped the mighty truth that God is one. Remember how men had to wait for centuries before the world was ready for Christ Jesus. Reflect that nineteen centuries have gone, and we seem only to be touching the hem of Christ's garment yet, and you will apprehend the leisureliness of heaven. In all God's dealings with the human race, and in all God's dealings with the human soul, there is purpose, urgency, infinite persistence; but I think no man will detect hurry there.

Now take our text and let it illuminate that thought. It is because God believes in man that He refuses to hurry his development. If there were no potentiality in human nature, no promise of a divine ideal at its core, a single season might be enough to ripen it, as it ripens the corn that rustles in the field. There are creatures that dance and die all in one summer's evening; and a summer's evening is long enough for them. But a thousand evenings are not enough for man, there is such promise in the sorriest life. When I think how long a little child is helpless, absolutely dependent on another's love; when I think of the slow stages of our growth up the steep slope to moral and spiritual manhood; when I remember that every vision that beckons us, and every hope that fires us, and every truth that illuminates and saves us, was won out of the riches of God, through the discipline and the chastisement of ages, I feel that the belief of God in man is wonderful: He hath believed in us, and therefore hath made no haste. We speak a great deal about our faith in God. Never forget God's glorious faith in us.

And when I pass to the earthly life of Jesus, I am arrested by the same procedure there. He was leisurely, just because He trusted men. He did not despair of them when they were backward; He did not reject them because they were slow to learn. When He had chosen a heart, He trained it with infinite patience, and just because He believed in it, He would not hurry. Compare His treatment of Judas with that of Peter. Christ did not believe in the sincerity of Judas. He knew him to be a hypocrite, and a traitor, and "what thou doest do quickly"—haste, get done with it! But Peter! Christ thoroughly believed in Peter. He saw the possibilities in Peter. He knew that underneath the sand, driven by the wind, there was bed-rock upon which to build a church. So Peter was allowed to go out into the night and to weep bitter tears under the look of Christ. There was no hurry. Let him weep his eyes out. Jesus believed in Peter, and let him alone. And Jesus was scourged and hung upon the cross, and lay in the grave, and rose on the third day, and the hours seemed endless to the fallen disciple, yet no word of comfort came from his Lord.

Then at long last, "Simon, son of Jonas, lovest thou Me?" "Yea, Lord, Thou knowest that I love Thee." The wheels of the chariot of Christ had tarried, just because He trusted that great heart of Peter.

Thus we come back to where we started from—the freedom from feverishness that is a mark of faith. Do you believe? Then the peace that passes understanding shall keep your heart and mind through Jesus Christ. Do you believe? Let me use a little illustration that may help to make clearer what I mean.

I notice that in these flimsy apartments which are being built in various quarters of the city, there is a great hurry to get all finished by the scheduled time. There is a feverish eagerness apparent to have everything ready and complete by Pentecost Sunday. But the old cathedrals were not build that way. The old cathedrals took hundreds of years to build. Men lived and died, and handed on the work, and there was plenty of time, for was not the work God's? And every finial and turret was perfected, for the builders said the "eyes of God were there." Are you not temples of the living God? Shall not the work go on through all eternity? Be zealous, strenuous! Give thy whole heart to things! "But he that believeth shall not make haste."

NOTES

Christian Faith and Christian Life

Samuel Porter Jones ("Sam Jones") (1847-1906) was an American evangelist who pastored Methodist churches in the South before launching out into evangelistic work. Before his conversion, he was failing as a lawyer, primarily because of a drink problem. His sermons were down-to-earth and his applications personal and practical. Like evangelist Billy Sunday, Jones strongly opposed the liquor business. This message is taken from the volume *Sam Jones* in "The Great Pulpit Masters" series published by Fleming H. Revell in 1950.

Sam Jones

11

CHRISTIAN FAITH AND CHRISTIAN LIFE

> Now, at about the midst of the feast, Jesus went up into the temple, and taught. And the Jews marveled, saying, How knoweth this man letters, having never learned? Jesus answered them, and said, My doctrine is not mine, but His that sent me. If any man will do His will, he shall know of the doctrine, whether it be of God, or whether I speak of myself (John 17:14-17).

AT THE TIME Jesus uttered these words He was surrounded by the sharp, calculating Sadducees and the shrewd, cunning Pharisees, and the probing, dissecting minds of the lawyers of His day. They were doubting; they were hating; they were despising; they were wondering. It is natural for man to doubt; it is very common for man to despise; and very frequently we are made to wonder at some things. It is as natural for a man to doubt as it is for him to live a sinner, and I suppose some of you find that very natural! A great many think, "Well, I am a sinner, because I am an infidel," but you are an infidel because you are a sinner. You have got the thing reversed. A man does not sin because he doubts; he doubts because he sins.

I believe the quickest, clearest, grandest conversion God had under His own immediate ministry was the case of Nathaniel. When Nathaniel came up into the presence of Christ, Christ dropped His finger on him and said: "Behold an Israelite indeed, in whom there is no guile!" (John 1:47).

And the doors of Nathaniel's heart flew wide open and he said "My Lord and my God." The quickest, clearest, grandest conversion of Jesus' ministry was the case of Nathaniel. He was without guile, and a heart without guile always opens itself when Christ is near.

Doubt Because of Sin

We sin, and we doubt because we sin. I said once before you never had a doubt in your life but that if you would take hold of it and pull it up by the roots you would find there was a seed at the bottom of the taproot, and the name of that seed is Sin. And if you will quit sinning, you will quit doubting just as naturally as possible.

Now, these scribes and Pharisees and lawyers stood around Christ, all probing, all despising, all wondering, and all were hypocrites. The Bible has a good deal to say about hypocrisy and about hypocrites, but nine-tenths of all the hypocrites I ever saw were out of the church. They do not belong to the church at all. When a man out there says he is as good as anybody, if he could get anybody to believe him he would be a first-class hypocrite, but his unreliability saves him from the charge of hypocrisy. Nobody believes him and therefore he passes for what he is worth. If that man out there could create the impression that he had done as much good as anybody he would be a first-class hypocrite. His failure to make the impression saves him from the charge of being a hypocrite.

Do you know what a hypocrite is? A hypocrite is a man that doesn't do right, but wants to make people believe he is doing right. It takes all these elements to make a hypocrite. Now, how many hypocrites do you know in the churches of this town that do not do right, who want to make people believe they do right, and who don't want to do right? How many hypocrites have you in the churches of your town, according to that rule? It is not so much whom you look at as it is what sort of a fellow is looking at you. There is a good deal in that. A dozen stood round looking at Christ, and Christ dropped His finger on them and said, "Whom say you—you, you and you—that I am?" And they said, "You are an impostor, and you are a blasphemer, and you are the son of—a harlot." And Jesus looked over to Peter, who was standing there, and said, "Peter, whom say ye I am?" I wish I could have seen Peter about that time. Just lifting his face up, he said: "Thou art the Christ, the Son of the living God" (Matthew 16:18). Peter was a man just like the rest of them, but Peter had got into a secret they did not know much about.

We say a man doubts only as he sins, and that he will

doubt as long as he is a sinner. But if you want to believe and believe with all your heart, empty your heart of guile, empty your heart of all sin, strip yourself of all this, and then you take in God for all He can do for a soul.

You have heard Christian people say, "Oh, I have so many doubts." Well, it is no credit to them. I will say that, and I would keep it to myself. You just size yourself up as a great big sinner if you have great big doubts. One is the result of the other.

"My Lord and my God" is the language of the man who saw Christ for the first time, and he took Christ into his soul the first time he had an opportunity. There is something very practical on the human side of salvation, whatever you may say about the mysteries on the other side, and I have noticed that the practical discharge of the duties God imposes on us makes a great many mysteries very plain to us. I have found that out.

Great Discoverers Have Met With Doubters

Now, I grant you that in all the ages of the world the great discoverers of this world have met with doubts and opposition, and frequently with doom. You may take Galileo, who asserted the discovery of Copernicus, that this world rotates on its axis. He was arraigned, tried, and convicted as the greatest heretic this world ever saw. And they laughed his theory to scorn and made him retract it, and yet when he walked out from that august body he turned and said: "And yet the world rolls on." And today any little schoolboy in this town will tell you that the world rotates on its axis and rolls round the sun in its yearly revolution. I believe every being in the universe has accepted the theory that the world moves round the sun.

When Harvey discovered that the blood circulated from the heart to the extremities and back again to the heart, he was arraigned by the world. They admitted that the earth rotated on its axis, but they would not admit that the blood circulated. They tried Harvey and convicted him as the greatest heretic this world ever saw. Yet now we honor him as one of earth's greatest discoverers, and today, when the physician walks into your sick room and lays his finger on your pulse, he determines the nature of the disease by the accelerated action of the pulse, which is the indicator of the arterial circulation. No one doubts now that the blood circulates.

When Isaac Watt discovered that steam—a bland vapor—had a power almost omnipotent, the world laughed him to scorn, and arraigned him, tried him, and convicted him as the greatest heretic the world ever saw. And when Stephenson constructed his engine, that infidel world stood and looked on, ready to laugh him to scorn; but when he pulled back the throttle and the engine moved off before the gaze of an infidel world with an astonishing power and velocity, the world hung its head. "We give up." Can anybody doubt the power of steam who sees these iron horses moving over this country a mile a minute, pulling their freighted tons over it? All opposition to this grand discoverer has died out with the past.

When Morse discovered that a man might chain electricity to a wire, and that one man might sit in one city and talk to a person in another city in private conversation, the world pricked up its ears and said, "We have a sure-enough humbug now, and we will condemn him without trial. It's the most astounding humbug the world ever saw; there is no truth in it." Who doubts now that I can go into a telegraph office in this town and talk for an hour to a friend in Liverpool, England? And I say of these grand discoverers who have proclaimed these discoveries to the world, that in this day the world builds monuments to them and honors them!

The Greatest Discoverer Has His Doubters

But the grandest discoverer in this world's history was He who 1,800 years ago discovered the balm of Gilead and poured His own precious blood out to redeem this world. That precious blood has been washing its millions for 1,800 years, and yet, today, after all the triumphs of the cross and the cleansing power of the blood, there is as much opposition from science today to the Christ crucified as there ever was in any age of the world. I reckon we would have been fighting Galileo today, if he had abused dram-drinking, cursing, and making money. I expect we would have been fighting Harvey on the same line. I expect we will fight anything that proposes to abridge our privileges to go to hell. Oh, why is it that we accept everything from everybody that is proven true, and yet when the blood-washed throng in heaven, and the best of earth stand up and testify to Jesus' power to save, there are those who have doubts and misgivings about His power to save a soul to God?

Thank God, 1,800 years ago, before I ever saw the light of this world, that precious blood was shed to redeem me, and thank God, 1,800 years after it was poured out my poor heart was washed in the blood Jesus Christ had poured out to save sinners. Now, I say this, and I talk with the Bible open before me, and with intelligent men and women before me. The science of Christ crucified, the religion of Christianity, may be tested just like anything else. A great many say it is a sentiment for old women and children. I recollect in the town where I lived that there was a poor fellow whom they called half-witted. All the sense he had in the world was religious sense, and all the sense he had was good sense—pious sense. And they used to dub him a crank and say he was carzy. They said he was crazy on the subject of religion, and I told the people they would all feel like there had been an eternal practical joke played on them, when they walked up the bar of God for judgment, to find that poor Gus, whom they had called crazy, was the only sensible man in the town. Let me say to those who speak of the religion of Jesus Christ as the plaything of an idiot, or as a sentiment for a poor old woman in her dotage to hug to her heart, that there is something in it to engage the grandest minds and keep busy the biggest hearts this world ever saw. Let us stop to think before we deride the religion that has blood-washed the world already and that proposes to save me and my child from the sins that beset us and make us meet and fit for the Master's house in heaven.

Now we stop for a moment. The science of mathematics, for instance, is a true science that has been demonstrated to be true. A man tells a class: "True it is that the science is true." I will say, "Demonstrate it to me." He says, "Twice two are four."

I say, "Hush, that is child's talk. Now demonstrate to me that mathematics is a true science."

And he says, "Six times six are thirty-six."

I say, "I do not want any foolishness. I want a grand demonstration that the science of mathematics is a true science."

He says, "You are a sensible man, and I will take you over here to these Alps," those grand mountains piled up there between France and Switzerland. Those two governments want to tunnel that mountain, and they want to begin on opposite sides of the mountain and meet each other in the middle of the mountain. Millions are involved in the undertaking, and the science of mathematics starts up and says, "I will guide you through that old dark mountain and bring you together in the heart of it." "But," say these governments, "if you fail to do it we have lost millions." The engineers say they will not fail, and they bring their instruments to bear on that old mountain and mark out the lines.

They work there for weeks, months and years, and thousands are spent, and people wonder how this is going to come out. One day the workmen on France's side sat down to dinner. The workmen on Switzerland's side rose from their midday meal and commenced work first. The French workmen suddenly heard the rumblings of the pick on the other side, and they jumped up and took up their tools and commenced work again on the partition of earth, and in fifteen minutes the middle wall fell out, and they had struck one another to the one-thousandth part of an inch. And there is one everlasting demonstration of the truth of the science of mathematics.

Christianity Is a True Science

Well, we say that Christianity may be tested just precisely like the science of mathematics may be tested.

It is a true science, and you can subject it to the most severe test and demonstrate it for yourself. That is it. Well, here is a man who declares it to be a true science, and says, "I believe in Jesus Christ."

"Well, what makes you believe in Jesus Christ?"

"Because He pardoned my sins."

"Oh, well, there may be a sentiment about that. I do not know about that. None of your foolishness, now. I want to know whether He is divine. I want to know whether He is God or not."

"I will tell you what I will do. Hunt me up a man born blind—one that never saw the light of this world, one whose eyes the doctors have failed to open. Get me a man born stone-blind, that never saw the light of day, and let me see him. Bring him out here. Let us give the world a demonstration that thou art God." Jesus calls the blind man up to Him, and He stoops down and spits on the ground, and makes clay with the spittle. And then He takes the clay and rubs it on the blind man's eyes, and He says, "Now, go and wash in yonder pool."

I expect if some of the scientific of our congregation had been there that day they would have said, "Look at that now, will you? He is making a fool of that poor fellow. Science demonstrates that there are curative properties in dry earth, but wet it, and the curative power is destroyed. To rub inert wet dirt on a man's eyes and tell him to go and wash his eyes in that pool—why, he has washed all over in that pool many a time—there is nothing in it." "Well," the poor, blind fellow says, "Don't you go on speculating. You can afford to speculate on this question, but it is a question of eyesight with me and I am going to try this thing. I heard what He said." And the blind man groped off in the darkness until he struck the edge of the pool, and then he stooped and pulled the water up to his eyes and washed the clay from his eyes and then wrung the water out of his eyes; and when he looked up he saw rocks, rivers and mountains that his eyes had never looked on before. The scientific gentlemen pressed around him, and said, "Look here, old fellow, we want to make something out of this case. We admit He has healed your eyes. We admit all that, but we want you to say He has got a devil."

The poor fellow looked up, with his eyes dancing in his head, and said, "I don't know whether He has a devil or not. I cannot tell you anything about that, but I know, 'whereas I was blind, now I see.' " And, brothers, there is demonstration for you.

"I like that. But can't you demonstrate it some other way?"

"Bring me up ten lepers this way"—and this old world had done its best on lepers in all of its ages, and admitted having done nothing.

They bring those ten lepers up to the Lord Jesus Christ, and they say, "Master, that we may be made whole." Jesus looked at the poor lepers, and said, "Go and show yourselves to the priest." The poor skeptics yonder say, "Mister, the priests won't let those lepers come around; they will hold up their hands, and tell them to keep off before anybody gets to them."

Oh, how ridiculous they make the poor lepers! Well, the lepers said, "You can argue with the Savior, but we're going to try this thing; we're going to the priest." Off they start, and before they got one hundred yards from the Son of God, one said, "The scales are falling from my body," and another said, "Such is the case with me," and one said, "I am sound from head to foot," and another said, "I am," and one ran back to praise God for the healing of all.

Do you want a better demonstration of the fact that God Almighty has power and strength to heal a man than when He does such things as these? Put it to the test—that's the question.

I'll tell you what's the matter with this old world. They don't want to test anything.

In this connection, this old world reminds me of a man standing down on the far side of the hill, and I say, "Friend, there is a bright light on the other side of the hill."

He says, "No, there ain't."

I say, "Well, come, I'll show you."

"I ain't going."

I catch him by the hand and I pull him along until I get to the top of the hill, where he can see the light, and as soon as he gets to where he can see the light he turns his head over so he can't see, and I turn his head back so he can see the light, and he shuts his eyes so he can't see. I pry his eyes open, and he says, "I don't want to see. It'll cost me something to see that light."

I say to a friend here in this town—he doesn't believe in railroads, he doesn't believe a locomotive can run a lick; he has looked at them, he has examined them; they weigh about forty tons, and he doesn't see how they can run—I say to him, "Well, friend, I have ridden on that train. It can run forty miles an hour. It can run from here to Nashville in eleven hours—340 miles."

"Oh, well," he says, "you can't fool me."

"Well," I say, "friend, there is something important in this move. I want to get you on my side, and now come down with me and I will show you."

"Well," he says, "I ain't got the money to spare."

"Well, I will pay your way. What do you say?"

"Well, I ain't going to. I don't believe it. The train don't move at all."

Now, you haven't the time to fool away with that fellow at all, have you?

And here is a grand science proposing to make the best for the universe, and we stand up prepared to prove what it has done, and that man stands up there and says practically on his lips, "I don't believe a word of it."

Now, you may test this thing. And when an infidel sits down and proposes to argue with me, I don't argue with him. I just ask him three questions, and when he gets through answering them the argument is closed, so far as I am concerned.

He says, "I don't believe Jesus Christ has power on earth to forgive sins."

I say, "Have you ever tried Him? Have you ever tried Him?"

"No."

"Well, will you try Him?"

"No."

"Well, will you acknowledge you are a fool?"

"No."

"Now, you see, we can't argue this thing any further. That just settles the matter right there."

"I have never tried Him, I am never going to try Hm, and I ain't a fool."

Now, when a man denies everything that you want to assert, then there is no ground there for an argument at all, and I just bid him good-by, and we go off, and I feel like I have done right, in that I have not wasted my time on a case like that.

"If any man will do His will, he shall know of the doctrine" (John 9:19). And when those scribes and Pharisees and hypocrites stood around Christ and were probing, dissecting and analyzing every word He said, Jesus turned around and threw the gauntlet down right at their feet, and said, to put the thing to the test, "And if you don't find it true, I will acknowledge myself an impostor and blasphemer in the sight of God and angels. What more do you want than that?" And I—if you will pardon the expression, I dare any man who doubts—I dare you to give up your sins and take Him who is a savior from sin as your portion.

God's Will for the Sinner

Now, it is important we stop right at this point and find out what is the will of God concerning a sinner.

Now, what is it? Peter learned at the feet of Jesus Himself what the duty of a sinner was. What did Peter say that day he had 3,000 converts under one sermon? He said: "Repent, ye, therefore, and be converted, that your sins may be blotted out. Repent! repent! repent!"

Now, brother, repentance is your part; salvation from sin is God's part with the world; and you need never expect God to do His part until you have done your part.

I heard of an old Hardshell once—he was not a converted Hardshell; he was an unconverted Hardshell—and that's the worst shape I have found the devil in yet. He was an unconverted Hardshell, and he would say, "What is to be is to be, you know," and he says, 'If you seek religion you can't find it, and if you find it you ain't got it, and if you've got it you can't lose it, and if you lose it you don't have it." And this is the way the world goes with him. But when you strike an Armenian sinner, a sinner who says, "I must do something; I must seek if I would find. I must knock if I would have the door opened. I must ask if I would receive," he says: "Well, thank God, if I seek religion, I'll find it, and if I find it, I've got it, and if I've got it I can lose it, and if I lose it, I've had it." And he works along on that plan. And, after all, brethren, I want to be the Armenian before I get religion, and a good Hardshell after I get it. Now, that is how I fix the thing. But God Almighty deliver me from Hardshellism before I get it. I am gone, certain. If I get to be a Hardshell before I get to be a Christian I am gone sure.

Now, this old Hardshell was about sixty years old. The preacher said: "We've got a good meeting; I wish you would come down to the meeting and give your heart to God." "Oh," said the Hardshell, "I have been listening for that still, small voice for sixty years." "Have you heard it?" "No." "Well, you're getting pretty deaf, and if you couldn't hear it when your ears were good, how do you expect to hear it now?" He told the old Hardshell: "You come to the meeting and seek God and you will find Him." And, to his astonishment, the old Hardshell was down at the altar and on his knees and praying that night. And next morning, before the service was concluded, the Hardshell was converted to God, and he stood up and slapped his hands together, and he said: "Brethren, I tell you that Methodism has done more for me in twelve hours than Hardshellism did for me in sixty years." He did, sure. And, now, we tell him, "if Methodism did that for you, you stay in it, and don't let the devil break in on you." That's my doctrine. But don't you try that thing on you until you get religion. If we seek Him we'll find Him, if we knock, it will be opened, and my duty is to repent. Repent and be converted. Repent of your sins and be turned around.

Be turned around! I have said before that there is but one road in the moral universe of God, and that one road goes to both worlds. I can take that street out there in front of this church and I can go to anywhere in the world I want to go. That road out there goes to everywhere—doesn't it? There is not a spot in America that I can't go to from that road out there. And, friends, every road is one road in the moral sense, and every Christian in this world is on the road to heaven, and every sinner is on the road to hell. The only difference between them at all is—here is heaven at that end of the road, and here is hell at this end, and the Christians are all going that way and the sinners all going this way; and it is not which road you are on, but which direction you are going.

I used to think that a fellow had to go a week's journey, and had to cross the hills and mountains and creeks and rivers and jump gullies and swim rivers. I thought it would take him a solid week to get to the road to heaven, but I found, at last, I had been on the road to hell all my life, and all I had to do to go to heaven was to turn around on the road I was on. As soon as you turn around, you are on the road to heaven as soon as anybody.

Old John Knight, of our Conference—Bishop (turning to Bishop Granberry, who was on the platform), you knew him—a saintly old man he was—was sitting back in the church one night listening to George Smith preach, and George was preaching on repentance, and he was agoing it. He was speaking of evangelical repentance and legal repentance, splitting hairs a mile long and quartering them, showing which was legal repentance and which was evangelical repentance, and old Uncle John Knight sat back there listening to old Uncle George until he was tired. Old Uncle John stood up and said: "George, won't you stop a minute and let me tell them what repentance is?" And George said, "Yes, Uncle John. I always like to hear you talk." Uncle John started up the aisle this way, and he said, "I am going to hell; I am going to hell; I am going to hell;" and when he got up to about the end of the aisle, he started right back, and he said, "I am going to heaven; I am going to heaven; I am going to heaven. "Now," said he, "George, tell 'em to turn around; that means repentance;

that means conversion; and don't stand there splitting hairs on evangelical and legal repentance."

God have mercy on us and show us that His will is that we be converted. And converted means nothing more than turning around. And when a man turns his back on sin and turns to God, he is as much on the road to heaven as any man in the universe. God help us to see that. If you want to go to heaven and are on the road to hell, just turn about. If you are on the way to heaven and you want to go to hell, Christian, just turn about. We have heaven at one end of the road and hell at the other. God help us, all of us, to turn our backs on sin, and then we have turned our backs on hell and our faces to heaven. And then let us move off. That is the will of God. That is it; that is it.

Oh, how I wish I could get five hundred persons tonight that are on the broad road just to see that all that God asks of them is to turn around. It is yours to turn around, and then it is God's to bring the times of refreshness on your soul. That is it.

Stand Up for the Right Thing

Now, I turn to another point here. The greatest man whose heart Christ ever touched was St. Paul. When Paul fell down before God the voice said: "Why persecutest Thou me?" And he said, "What wilt Thou have me to do?" . . . And the Lord said to him, "Rise, stand upon thy feet" (Acts 9:4-6).

Brother, the first thing a man ought to do is to get up from a life of sin and take a stand for the right. "I will take a stand." That's it. St. Paul put it afterward in this shape: "I fought a good fight." And when St. Paul said, "I fought a good fight," he said two things in that one sentence with a vengeance. First, "I got over on the good side;" second, "I have fought with all my ransomed powers." First, get over on the good side, and when he is clear over, I want a fellow to get so far over the line that if he wants to fall over the line his head will not fall within ten feet of it. If he falls over, I want him to fall clear over.

A Christian has no right in the devil's territory.

A fellow says: "I go in a barroom because I got business in there." But what business has a Christian got in there? That's the mystery to me.

"Well, I go in there to collect my rents."

Yes, yes; and I'll risk the barkeeper's chances of heaven before I'll risk yours, you old hypocrite, you! You understand that? The barkeepers and whisky men are not the meanest men in this town. But if you can find me a member of the church that runs a house and rents a place of business for them, I will show you a man that is not only as mean as a barkeeper in every other respect, but adds to it the sin of hypocrisy.

I say, let a man stay on God's territory if he is a Christian, and let him stand there with his weapons drawn, and let him fight for the right.

I saw some time ago where a young lady member of the church went to a ball and danced, and died in the ballroom. It was said further that after a few minutes the devil came right in and gathered up her soul and started off with it. A few minutes more and St. Peter came along, and he saw that a Christian, a member of the church, had died, and he said: "Where's the soul of the member of the church?"

They said: "The devil has just carried it off."

"Well, how long has it been gone?"

"Oh, just a few minutes; not long."

And St. Peter started off at breakneck speed and said he would overtake that soul and the devil shouldn't have it. It was a Christian soul, he said, and away he ran, and presently he overtook the devil, and said: "Hold! Hold on there! You made a mistake this time!"

"What?" said the devil.

"Why, you've got the soul of that girl, and she's a Christian."

"Well," said the devil, "I didn't know that. I got her over in my territory and I reckon she's mine."

Well, now, you can't afford to run over on the devil's side. Anyhow, you'd better mind how you die over there. I want to get back before I die. St. Paul said: "I have fought a good fight." And by that he meant: "I have come over. I have taken a stand on God's side." And when a man takes his stand on God's side the powers of hell rush upon him, almost before he has time to draw his sword. It is like John Bunyan pictures it in his *Pilgrim's Progress,* when his pilgrim is in the Interpreter's house:

> I saw, also, that the Interpreter took him again by the hand and led him into a pleasant place, where was built a stately palace, beautiful to behold, at the sight of which Christian was greatly delighted. He saw, also, upon the top thereof certain persons walking, who were clothed all in gold.
>
> And the Interpreter took him and led him up toward the door of the palace; and, behold, at the door stood a great company of men, as desirous to go in, but durst not. There also sat a man a little distance from the door, at a tableside, with a book and his inkhorn before him, to take the name of him that should enter therein. He saw also that in the doorway stood many men in armor to keep it, being resolved to do the men that would enter what hurt and mischief they could. Now was Christian somewhat in amaze.
>
> At last, when every man started back for fear of the armed men, Christian saw a man of a very stout countenance come up to the man that sat there to write, saying: "Set down my name, sir."
>
> And when he had done this he saw the man draw his sword and put a helmet upon his head and rush toward the door upon the armed men, who laid upon him with deadly force. But the man, not at all discouraged, fell to cutting and hacking most fiercely. So after he had received and given many wounds to those that attempted to keep him out, he cut his way through them all, and pressed forward into the palace, at which there was a pleasant voice heard from those that were within, even of those that walked upon the top of the palace, saying:
>
> "Come in! Come in!
> Eternal glory thou shalt win."
>
> So he went in and was clothed with such garments as they.

And so with you. After you have fought the good fight, and steel has clanged against steel, and you have warded off blow after blow, and dealt stroke after stroke upon the enemy, until your worn-out blade drops from your nerveless hand, God shall say to you: "Come up higher. You have fought the good fight, and I have helped you! You have conquered and I will crown you."

And heaven is just the other side of the hardest battle man ever fought in the world.

Take a stand for God and the right!

What is the will of God concerning me? Peter said, "Repent and be converted." God said to Paul, "Arise! Stand on your feet."

Take a stand! Take a stand! I have never yet known a Christian man—a man who wanted to be a Christian—to take a stand that God didn't come to him.

Take a stand! I have never yet known a soul to eschew evil and say, "I take a stand for the right," that God didn't come to him.

Sir, what is the will of God concerning me?

Listen just a moment! It is to give up evil and take a stand for the right. Are you willing to do that? There's something very practical about that, brother. Listen: "If any man will do the will of God, he shall know of the doctrine." That is, know it for himself. And then I would have you notice another fact in the text: "If any man—".

That looks in the face a whole world of human beings and points its finger at each one of you and says: "If you, if you, sir—if you, sir, do what God tells you to do, you shall know of the doctrine, whether it be of God or whether Christ spoke it of himself." That's the text.

And I tell you another thing. I'm never troubled with any doubts when I'm doing the will of God. I'm never troubled with any doubts when I'm doing what God tells me to do, and every doubt I have ever had was when I had refused to do something God told me to do, or else I willingly lent myself to evil influences.

NOTES

Walking By Sight or Walking By Faith

John Wesley (1703-1791), along with his brother Charles, and George Whitefield, founded the Methodist movement in Britain and America. On May 24, 1738, he had his great spiritual experience in a meeting at Aldersgate Street, when his "heart was strangely warmed" and he received assurance of salvation. Encouraged by Whitefield to do open-air preaching, Wesley soon was addressing thousands, in spite of the fact that many churches were closed to him. The Methodist "societies" that he formed became local churches that conserved the results of his evangelism. He wrote many books and preached 40,000 sermons during his long ministry. This one is taken from volume 7 of the *Complete Works* published by Zondervan Publishing House, and was preached in London on December 30, 1788.

John Wesley

12

WALKING BY SIGHT OR WALKING BY FAITH

We walk by faith, not by sight (2 Corinthians 5:7).

HOW SHORT IS this description of real Christians! And yet how exceeding full! It comprehends, it sums up, the whole experience of those that are truly such, from the time they are born of God till they remove into Abraham's bosom. For, who are the *we* that are here spoken of? All that are true Christian believers. I say *Christian,* not *Jewish,* believers. All that are not only *servants,* but *children,* of God. All that have "the Spirit of adoption, crying in their hearts, Abba, Father" (Romans 8:15). All that have "the Spirit of God witnessing with their spirits, that they are the sons of God."

All these, and these alone, can say, "We walk by faith, and not by sight." But before we can possibly "walk by faith," we must *live* by faith, and not by sight. And to all real Christians our Lord saith, "Because I live, ye live also" (John 14:19). Ye live a life which the world, whether learned or unlearned, "know not of." "You that," like the world, "were dead in trespasses and sins, hath he quickened," and made alive, given you new senses—spiritual senses—, "senses exercised to discern spiritual good and evil."

In order thoroughly to understand this important truth, it may be proper to consider the whole matter. All the children of men that are not born of God "walk by sight," having no higher principle. By *sight,* that is, by *sense;* a part being put for the whole; the sight for all the senses; the rather, because it is more noble and more extensive than any, or all the rest. There are but few objects we can discern by the three inferior senses of taste, smell, and feeling; and none of these can take any cognizance of its object, unless it be brought into a direct contact with it. Hearing, it is true, has a larger sphere of action, and gives us some knowledge of things that are distant. But how small is that distance, suppose it were fifty or a hundred miles, compared to that between the earth and the sun! And what is even this in comparison of the distance of the sun and moon and the fixed stars! Yet the sight continually takes knowledge of objects even at this amazing distance.

By sight we take knowledge of the visible world, from the surface of the earth to the region of the fixed stars. But what is the world visible to us, but "a speck of creation," compared to the whole universe?, to the invisible world?—that part of the creation which we cannot see at all, by reason of its distance; in the place of which, through the imperfection of our senses, we are presented with an universal blank.

But beside these innumerable objects which we cannot see by reason of their distance, have we not sufficient ground to believe that there are innumerable others of too delicate a nature to be discerned by any of our senses? Do not all men of unprejudiced reason allow the same thing (the small number of Materialists, or Atheists, I cannot term *men of reason*), that there is an invisible world, naturally such, as well as a visible one? But which of our senses is fine enough to take the least knowledge of this? We can no more perceive any part of this by our sight, than by our feeling. Should we allow, with the ancient poet, that

> Millions of spiritual creatures walk the earth
> Unseen, both when we wake, and when we sleep;

should we allow, that the great Spirit, the Father of all, filleth both heaven and earth; yet is the finest of our senses utterly incapable of perceiving either Him or them.

All our external senses are evidently adapted to this external, visible world. They are designed to serve us only while we sojourn here, while we dwell in these houses of clay. They have nothing to do with the invisible world; they are not adapted to it. And they can take no more cognizance of the eternal, than of the invisible world; although we are as fully assured of the existence of this, as of anything in the present world. We cannot think death puts a period to our being. The body indeed returns to dust; but the soul, being of a nobler nature, is not affected thereby. There is, therefore, an eternal world, of what kind soever it be. But how shall we attain the knowledge of this? What will teach us to draw aside the veil "that hangs 'twixt mortal and immortal being?" We all know, "the vast, the unbounded prospect lies before us;" but we are constrained to add, "Yet clouds, alas! and darkness rest upon it."

The most excellent of our senses, it is undeniably plain, can give us no assistance herein. And what can our boasted reason do? It is now universally allowed, *Nihil est in intellectu quod non fuit prius in sensu* (Nothing is in the understanding, which was not first perceived by some of the senses). Consequently, the understanding, having here nothing to work upon, can afford us no help at all. So that, in spite of all the information we can gain, either from sense or reason, both the invisible and eternal world are unknown to all that "walk by sight."

But is there no help? Must they remain in total darkness concerning the invisible and the eternal world? We cannot affirm this. Even the heathens did not all remain in total darkness concerning them. Some few rays of light have, in all ages and nations, gleamed through the shade. Some light they derived from various fountains touching the invisible world. "The heavens declared the glory of God," though not to their outward sight: "The firmament showed," to the eyes of their understanding, the existence of their Maker. From the creation they inferred the being of a Creator, powerful and wise, just and merciful. And hence they concluded, there must be an eternal world, a future state, to commence after the present; wherein the justice of God in punishing wicked men, and his mercy in rewarding the righteous, will be openly and undeniably displayed in the sight of all intelligent creatures.

We may likewise reasonably suppose, that some traces of knowledge, both with regard to the invisible and the eternal world, were delivered down from Noah and his children, both to their immediate and remote descendants. And, however these were obscured or disguised by the addition of numberless fables, yet something of truth was still mingled with them, and these streaks of light prevented utter darkness. Add to this, that God never, in any age or nation, "left himself" quite "without a witness" in the hearts of men; but while he "gave them rain and fruitful seasons," imparted some imperfect knowledge of the Giver. "He is the true Light that" still, in some degree, "enlighteneth every man that cometh into the world."

But all these lights put together availed no farther than to produce a faint twilight. It gave them, even the most enlightened of them, no *demonstration,* no *demonstrative conviction,* either of the invisible or of the eternal world. Our philosophical poet justly terms Socrates, "The wisest of all moral men;" that is, of all that were not favored with Divine Revelation. Yet what evidence had he of another world when he addressed those that had condemned him to death?—"And now, O ye judges, ye are going to live, and I am going to die. Which of these is best, God knows; but I suppose no man does." Alas! What a confession is this! Is this all the evidence that poor dying Socrates had either of an invisible or an eternal world? And yet even this is preferable to the light of the great and good Emperor Adrian. Remember, ye modern heathens, and copy after his pathetic address to his parting soul. For fear I should puzzle you with Latin, I give it you in Prior's fine translation:

> Poor, little, pretty, fluttering thing,
> Must we no longer live together?
> And dost thou prune thy trembling wing,
> To take thy flight, thou know'st not whither?
> Thy pleasing vein, thy humorous folly,
> Lies all neglected, all forgot!
> And pensive, wavering, melancholy,
> Thou hop'st and fear'st, thou know'st not what.

"Thou know'st not what!" True, there was no knowledge of what was to be hoped or feared after death, till "the Sun of Righteousness" arose to dispel all their vain conjectures, and "brought life and immortality," that is, immortal life, "to light, through the Gospel." Then (and not till then, unless in some rare instances) God revealed, unveiled the invisible world. He then revealed himself to the children of men. "The Father revealed the Son" in their hearts; and the Son revealed the Father. He that of old time "commanded light to shine out of darkness shined in their hearts, and enlightened them with the knowledge of the glory of God in the face of Jesus Christ."

It is where sense can be of no farther use, that faith comes in to our help; it is the grand *desideratum;* it does what none of the senses can; no, not with all the helps that art hath invented. All our instruments, however improved by the skill and labor of so many succeeding ages, do not enable us to make the least discovery of these unknown regions. They barely serve the occasions for which they were formed in the present visible world.

How different is the case, how vast the pre-eminence, of them that "walk by faith!" God, having "opened the eyes of their understanding," pours divine light into their soul; whereby they are enabled to "see Him that is invisible," to see God and the things of God. What their "eye had not seen, nor their ear heard, neither had it entered into their heart to conceive," God from time to time reveals to them by the "unction of the Holy One, which teacheth them of all things." Having "entered into the holiest by the blood of Jesus," by that "new and living way," and being joined unto "the general assembly and church of the first-born, and unto God the Judge of all, and Jesus the Mediator of the New Covenant,"—each of these can say, "I live not, but Christ liveth in me;" I now live that life which "is hid with Christ in God;" "and when Christ, who is *my* life, shall appear, then *I* shall likewise appear with him in glory" (Colossians 3:4).

They that *live* by faith, *walk by faith.* But what is implied in this? They regulate all their judgments concerning good and evil, not with reference to visible and temporal things, but things invisible and eternal. They think visible things to be of small value, because they pass away like a dream; but, on the contrary, they account invisible things to be of high value, because they will never pass away. Whatever is invisible is eternal; the things that are not seen, do not perish. So the apostle Paul: "The things which are seen are temporal, but the things which are not seen are eternal" (2 Corinthians 4:18). Therefore, they that "walk by faith" do not desire the "things which are seen;" neither are they the object of their pursuit. They "set their affection on things above, not on things on the earth." They seek only the things which are "where Jesus sitteth at the right hand of God." Because they know, "the things that are seen are temporal," passing away like a shadow, therefore they "look not at them;" they desire them not; they account them as nothing; but "they look at the things which are not seen, that are eternal," that never pass away. By these they form their judgments of all things. They judge them to be good or evil, as they promote or hinder their welfare, not in time, but in eternity. They weigh whatever occurs in this balance: "What influence has it on my eternal state?" They regulate all their tempers and passions, all their desires, joys, and fears, by this standard. They regulate all their thoughts and designs, all their words and actions, so as to prepare them for that invisible and eternal world to which they are shortly going. They do not *dwell* but only *sojourn* here; not looking upon earth as their home, but only

> Travelling through Immanuel's ground,
> To fairer worlds on high.

Brethren, are *you* of this number, who are now here before God? Do *you* see "Him that is invisible?" Have you faith, living faith, the faith of a child? Can you say, "The life that I now live, I live by faith in the Son of God, who loved me, and gave Himself for me?" Do you "walk by faith?" Observe the question. I do not ask, whether you curse, or swear, or profane the Sabbath, or live in any outward sin. I do not ask, whether you do good, more or less; or obey all the commandments of God. But, suppose you are blameless in all these respects, I ask, in the name of God, by what standard do you judge the value of things? By the visible or the invisible world? Bring the matter to an issue in a single instance. Which do you judge best, that your son should be a pious cobbler, or a profane lord? Which appears to you most eligible, that your daughter should be a child of God, and walk on foot, or a child of the devil, and ride in a coach-and-six? When the question is concerning marrying your daughter, if you consider her body more than her soul, take knowledge of yourself: You are in the way to hell, and not to heaven; for you walk by sight, and not by faith. I do not ask, whether you live in any outward sin or neglect; but, do you *seek,* in the general tenor of your life, "the things that are above," or the things that are below? Do you "set your affection on things above," or on "things of the earth?" If on the latter, you are as surely in the way of destruction, as a thief or a common drunkard. My dear friends, let every man, every woman among you, deal honestly with yourselves. Ask your own heart, "What am I seeking day by day? What am I desiring? What am I pursuing? Earth or heaven? The things that are seen, or the things that are not seen?" What is your object, God or the world? As the Lord liveth, if the world is your object, still all your religion is vain.

See then, my dear brethren, that from this time, at least, ye choose the better part. Let your judgment of all the things round about you be according to the real value of things, with reference to the invisible and eternal world. See that ye judge everything fit to be pursued or shunned, according to the influence it will have on your eternal state. See that your affections, your desire, your joy, your hope, be set, not on transient objects, not on things that fly as a shadow, that pass away like a dream; but on those that are incapable of change, that are incorruptible and fade not away; those that remain the same, when heaven and earth "flee away, and there is no place found for them." See that in all you think, speak, or do, the eye of your soul be single, fixed on "Him that is invisible," and "the glories that shall be revealed." Then shall "your whole body be full of light." Your whole soul shall enjoy the light of God's countenance; and you shall continually see the light of the glorious love of God "in the face of Jesus Christ."

See, in particular, that all your "desire be unto him, and unto the remembrance of his name." Beware of "foolish and hurtful desires;" such as arise from any visible or temporal thing. All these John warns us of, under that general term, "love of the world." It is not so much to the men of the world, as to the children of God, he gives that important direction: "Love not the world, neither the things of the world." Give no place to the "desire of the flesh,"—the gratification of the outward senses, whether of the taste, or any other. Give no place to "the desire of the eye"—the internal sense, or imagination—by gratifying it, either by grand things, or beautiful, or uncommon. Give no place to the "pride of life," the desire of wealth, of pomp, or of the honor that cometh of men. John confirms this advice, by a consideration parallel to that observation which Paul had made to the Corinthians, "for the world and the fashion of it passeth away." "The fashion of it"—all worldly objects, business, pleasures, cares, whatever now attracts our regard or attention—"passeth away,"—is in the very act of passing, and will return no more. Therefore, desire none of these fleeting things, but that glory which "abideth for ever."

This is religion, and this alone; this alone is true Christian religion; not this or that opinion, or system of opinions, be they ever so true, ever so scriptural. It is true, this is commonly called faith. But those who suppose it to be religion are given up to a strong delusion to believe a lie, and if they suppose it to be a sure passport to heaven are in the high road to hell. Observe well that religion is not harmlessness; which a careful observer of mankind properly terms *hellish harmlessness,* as it sends thousands to the bottomless pit. It is not *morality;* excellent as that is, when it is built on a right foundation,—loving faith; but when otherwise, it is of no value in the sight of God. It is not *formality,* the most exact observance of all the ordinances of God. This, too, unless it be built on the right foundation, is no more pleasing to God, than "the cutting off a dog's neck." No, religion is no less than living in eternity, and walking in eternity; and hereby walking in the love of God and man, in lowliness, meekness, and resignation. This, and this alone, is that "life which is hid with Christ in God." He alone who experiences this "dwells in God, and God in him." This alone is setting the crown upon Christ's head, and doing his "will on earth as it is done in heaven."

It will easily be observed, that this is the very thing that men of the world call enthusiasm, a word just fit for their purpose, because no man can tell either the meaning or even the derivation of it. If it has any determinate sense, it means a species of religious madness. Hence, when you speak your experience, they immediately cry out, "Much religion hath made thee mad." And all that you experience, either of the invisible or of the eternal world, they suppose to be only the waking dreams of a heated imagination. It cannot be otherwise, when men born blind take upon them to reason concerning light and colors. They will readily pronounce those to be insane who affirm the existence of those things whereof they have no conception.

From all that has been said, it may be seen, with the utmost clearness, what is the nature of that fashionable thing called *dissipation.* He that hath ears to hear, let him hear! It is the very quintessence of Atheism; it is artificial, added to natural, ungodliness. It is the art of forgetting God, of being altogether "without God in the world;" the art of excluding him, if not out of the world he has created, yet out of the minds of all his intelligent creatures. It is a total studied inattention to the whole invisible and eternal world; more especially to death, the gate of eternity, and to the important consequences of death,—heaven and hell!

This is the real nature of *dissipation.* And is it so harmless a thing as it is usually thought? It is one of the choicest instruments of destroying immortal spirits that was ever forged in the magazines of hell. It has been the means of plunging myriads of souls, that might have enjoyed the glory of God, into the everlasting fire prepared for the devil and his angels. It blots out all religion at one stroke, and levels man with the beasts that perish. All ye that fear God, flee from dissipation! Dread and abhor the very name of it! Labor to have God in all your thoughts, to have eternity ever in your eye! "Look" continually, "not at the things that are seen, but at the things which are not seen." Let your hearts be fixed there, where "Christ sitteth at the right hand of God!" that whensoever He calleth you, "an entrance may be ministered unto you abundantly into His everlasting kingdom!"

NOTES

CLASSIC SERMONS ON PRAYER

compiled by Warren W. Wiersbe

Prayer is the lifeline of the Christian. Only through an active prayer life can there by real spiritual growth.

Fourteen pulpit giants present the need, the how-to, and the results of a life that is permeated with prayer. These classic sermons on prayer will energize your prayer life, show you how to expect great things from God, and help you experience the strengthening power of God in your everyday life.

The great sermons in this volume are by such famous preachers as: Dwight L. Moody, G. Campbell Morgan, Charles H. Spurgeon, Rueben A. Torrey, Alexander Whyte, and others.

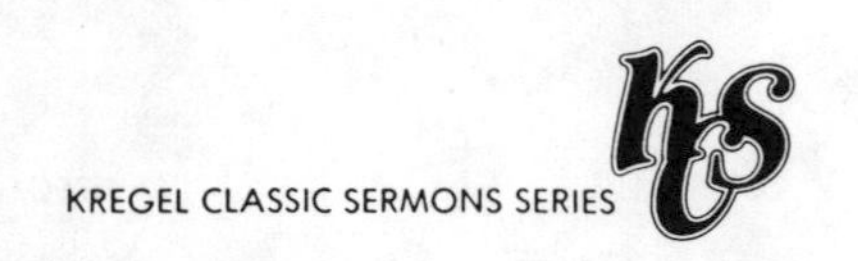

CLASSIC SERMONS ON FAITH AND DOUBT

compiled by Warren W. Wiersbe

Twelve pulpit giants give you inspiration and devotional challenge for your faith in this book of sermons. These messages to stimulate your faith are from the pulpit ministry of John W. Jowett, D. Martyn Lloyd-Jones, G. Campbell Morgan, Martin Luther, John Wesley and others. They will inevitably make your spiritual faith to grow into a strong and vibrant faith of maturity. Preachers and lay persons alike will be encouraged and find great blessing in these forceful messages.

CLASSIC SERMONS ON SUFFERING

Let the pulpit giants provide your resource material for words of comfort and solace. A master preacher in his own right, Warren W. Wiersbe, compiled these sixteen sermons by Phillips Brooks, John Calvin, Walter A. Maier, Charles H. Spurgeon, George W. Truett and others to offer perspective and understanding and to uplift the depressed and broken-hearted.

These *Classic Sermons on Suffering* will undergird your faith and focus your attention upon Christ, our great High Priest, who can "be touched with the feeling of our infirmities." Preachers will gain inspiration, ideas and insight to improve their ministry to those who suffer.

TREASURY OF THE WORLD'S GREATEST SERMONS

123 Sermons by 123 of the world's most notable preachers of ancient and modern days

A Sermon Library in One Volume

compiled by Warren W. Wiersbe

The various pulpit princes and their sermon masterpieces are organized and presented here, together with dates and indexes of authors, sermon topics and Bible texts. They illustrate variety of gift, diversity of method, together with national and ecclesiastical peculiarities.

This list of great preachers include among others: theologians like John Calvin and Jonathan Edwards; evangelists like Christmas Evans; and pulpiteers like Charles H. Spurgeon, G. Campbell Morgan, and Alexander Maclaren.

Progress is shown in the art of preaching. Although all have literary and rhetorical excellence, each sermon contains a distinct message helpful in solving some present-day problem in Christian living. Each one is fairly representative of the preaching that characterized the age to which it respectively belongs.

"Every minister should be a reader," writes Warren W. Wiersbe. Himself an ardent reader of sermons and biographies, he recommends that every minister read the giants, writers and preachers of all centuries, both what they have written and their biographies.

For variety and solid content, the *Treasury of the World's Great Sermons* is a superior collection.

